TABOO:
"THE ECSTASY OF EVIL"
THE PSYCHOPATHOLOGY
OF SEX AND RELIGION

Notice And Disclaimer
The case histories of this book are real and so are the religious Orders and Groups referred to. However, for the protection of these Orders and to safeguard the privacy of the individuals involved some people are presented as composite characters and the sequence of events and places have been suitably adapted.

TABOO:
"THE ECSTASY OF EVIL"
THE PSYCHOPATHOLOGY OF SEX AND RELIGION

By
Christopher S. Hyatt, Ph.D.
Lon Milo DuQuette
Gary Ford

Introduced By
Robert Anton Wilson, Ph.D.

1991
NEW FALCON PUBLICATIONS
SCOTTSDALE, ARIZONA U.S.A.

COPYRIGHT 1991 © USESS

All rights reserved. No part of this book, in part or in whole, may be reproduced, transmitted, or utilized, in any form or by any means, electronic or mechanical, including photocopying, recording, or by any information storage and retrieval system, without permission in writing from the publisher, except for brief quotations in critical articles, books and reviews.

International Standard Book Number: 1-56184-039-4

First Edition 1991

Cover by Linda Miller

NEW FALCON PUBLICATIONS
7025 E. 1st Ave. Suite 5
Scottsdale, Arizona 85251 U.S.A.
(602) 246-3546

Acknowledgements
For Research And Editing
Nick Tharcher
J. T. Boyer
Colleen Ford
J. Wilson
David P. Wilson
and to all those who requested
that their name be withheld

OTHER CONTROVERSIAL BOOKS FROM NEW FALCON

Equinox Of The Gods
Eight Lectures On Yoga
Gems From The Equinox
Magick Without Tears
The Worlds Tragedy
The Law Is For All
The Heart Of The Master
Little Essays Toward Truth
   By Aleister Crowley
Undoing Yourself With Energized Meditation
Secrets of Western Tantra
The Tree Of Lies
   By Christopher S. Hyatt, Ph.D.
Enochian World Of Aleister Crowley: Enochian Sex Magick
   By Aleister Crowley • Lon M. DuQuette • C. S. Hyatt
The Way Of The Secret Lover: Tantra, Tarot & The HGA
   By Christopher S. Hyatt, Ph.D. • Lon Milo DuQuette
Taboo: The Ecstasy Of Evil
   By C. S. Hyatt, Ph.D. • Lon DuQuette • Gary Ford
The Illustrated Goetia: Sex Magick And Evocation
   By Lon Milo DuQuette • C.S. Hyatt, Ph.D. • David P. Wilson
The Serpent, The Beast And The Golden Dawn
   By C. S. Hyatt, Ph.D. • Gary Ford • Lon DuQuette
Freedom Is A Two Edged Sword
   By Jack Parsons
Cosmic Trigger I & II
Sex And Drugs
   By Robert Anton Wilson
Info-Psychology
   By Timothy Leary, Ph.D.
The Complete Golden Dawn System Of Magic
   By Israel Regardie

And to get your free catalog of all of our titles, write to:

NEW FALCON PUBLICATIONS
Catalog Dept.
7025 E. 1ST. Ave. Suite 5
SCOTTSDALE, AZ. 85251 U.S.A.

Table of Contents

Introduction
 By Robert Anton Wilson 9
Chapter One
 Thou Shalt Not… 15
Chapter Two
 The Black Beauty And The Priest 27
Chapter Three
 Damned If You Do 31
Chapter Four
 It's So Holy It's Dirty 33
Chapter Five
 Sex And Religion 37
Chapter Six
 When Religion Was Sex 41
Chapter Seven
 Sex Among The Puffers 49
Chapter Eight
 The Devil You Say 53
Chapter Nine
 The Vampire 57
Chapter Ten
 Incuibi And Succubi: Demonic Sexual Violation 61
Chapter Eleven
 Magickal Children 69
Chapter Twelve
 Orgasm And Genetic Ecology 73
Chapter Thirteen
 The Black Mass 79
Chapter Fourteen
 Magick Menses 81

Chapter Fifteen
  Sperm As A "Drug" 85
Chapter Sixteen
  The Elixir Of Life 87
Chapter Seventeen
  The Eucharist And The Elixir Of Life 91
Chapter Eighteen
  The Talisman: Making The Dead Live 95
Chapter Nineteen
  The Sex Magician 99
Chapter Twenty
  Of Eating Blood And Idol Worship 101
Section II
  Modern Sex Magicians • Secret Sex Rituals 105
Chapter Twenty One
  The Knights Templar And The Sex Magicians 107
Chapter Twenty Two
  Aleister Crowley: Wickedest Man In The World? 111
Chapter Twenty Three
  The Bloody Sacrifice 117
Chapter Twenty Four
  Energized Enthusiasm 129
Chapter Twenty Five
  The Secret Of The Holy Graal 153
Chapter Twenty Six
  Sexual Alchemy 159
Chapter Twenty Seven
  Occult Eugenics 173
Chapter Twenty Eight
  The Royal Mass Of The Secret Lover 185
Chapter Twenty Nine
  Mystical/Magickal Meaning Of The Royal Mass 195

Chapter Thirty
  The Ceremony Of The Sun And Moon 199
Chapter Thirty One
  Angelic Sex Magick 209
Chapter Thirty Two
  Techniques Of Enochian Sex Magick 215
Chapter Thirty Three
  Biblical Erotica 229

INTRODUCTION

by Robert Anton Wilson

> You cannot kill time without
> injuring eternity.
> —Adam Weishaupt

When Playboy Press was about to publish my second book, *Sex and Drugs,* I asked Alan Watts to send them a jacket blurb. He wrote a letter to Playboy, saying "This obscene, lewd, blasphemous, subversive and very interesting book should be banned, bowdlerized, censored, suppressed and burned by the public hangman." On a xerox to me, he added "This ought to help you sell a million copies!" The editors at the Bunny Empire did not agree with Alan's whimsical approach to controversy in advertising. All they quoted on the jacket was "very interesting—Alan Watts."

Well, maybe Falcon has more wit and more intelligence than the Rabbit Warren. I assure you that what you are about to read is obscene, lewd, blasphemous, subversive and very interesting, and that all right-thinking people will agree that it should be banned, bowdlerized, censored, suppressed and burned by the public hangman.

Of course, you will think I am joking.

Well...There is a clergyman at large in this great nation who claims that Mister Ed, the talking horse on the TV comedy, is the Great Beast foretold in the last book of the Bible. Is this rev. gentlemen joking? Are you quite sure about that? Don't be too sure about me, either. Sometimes the Mysteries have to be approached—ah—on all fours, as it were.

Taboo: The Ecstasy Of Evil

For instance, I recently read a most interesting novel called *This'll Kill Ya,* by Harry Willson (no relative.) The cover warned me, and every chapter in the book repeated the warning:

CAUTION! READING THIS BOOK MAY BE HAZARDOUS TO YOUR HEALTH!

The plot concerned a book which allegedly kills people. The policeman investigating this book is, naturally, a bit cautious once he gets his hands on a copy of the loathsome and fearful volume. The reader also tends to become cautious, after a while, since it soon becomes obvious that the book you are reading is the book you are *reading about*—the book that can kill people, which is called *This'll Kill Ya...*

Fortunately, the book will only kill you if share the most common superstition in our culture—the idea that words on paper can be dangerous. In other words, the more deeply you fear certain ideas, images and taboo topics generally, the more likely it is that the book, *This'll Kill Ya,* might in fact kill ya.

Here we confront a terrible paradox like unto the divinely revealed Hell Laws of the Discordian religion, which hold that (1) Hell only exists for those who believe Hell exists and (2) the worst part of Hell is reserved for those who believe in Hell because they think they'll go there if they don't believe in it.

Who, then, by extension of the Hell Laws, stands in most dire danger from *This'll Kill Ya?* Those who believe that words on paper—or words on radio or TV or computernets—can be dangerous, and that therefore certain words should be banned, bowdlerized, censored, suppressed and maybe even burned by the public hangman. But people who believe in this diabolical power of words and/or ideas and/or images are precisely the people who form censorship societies, and study new books or other forms of art, science or entertainment, and decide which are dangerous. In short, *This'll Kill Ya* is most to prove fatal precisely to those who think it might be fatal.

You see, after decades of mulling this mystery—why are some people so terrified of certain words and ideas—I think I finally found the answer in the 18th Century Neapolitan sociologist Giambatista Vico, best known today as the inventor of what we now call transpersonal linguistics. Vico had lots of other ideas, however, but wrote them in rather opaque language—in Naples, at that time, the Holy Inquisition still occasionally toasted people who had original notions.

Vico seems to imply, in his indirect Neapolitan way, that the first god was the thunder, and morality derives from traumatic experiences with thunder (i.e. "negative imprints.") Vico was the first to study the cave peoples, and to suggest Bigfoot was a survivor of that age—and from cave art he deduced that anything that happened just before thunder was construed by them as arousing the anger of the thunder-god.

Thus, imagine some cave man about to clunk his brother on the head with an axe, when the thunder crashed. For the next 30,000 years we have kept the taboo, "Never kill members of your own tribe." War goes on, because in those early days the thunder never struck when somebody was getting ready to hit a "foreigner" (non-tribe-member) with an axe.

Similarly, some delightful sexual dalliances got put under Big Taboo, because just "Well, we can't do it that way after all." Another taboo lasted 30,000 years or longer...

In some cases, nobody could figure out what had provoked the anger of the sky-god—why the thunder roared at a certain moment. The early shamans must have given this a lot of thought. They finally decided that since nothing had happened, the god must have gotten royally pissed off at something somebody **said.** And so, bit by bit, or byte by byte, more and more ideas and images were denied verbal expression, because the thunder-god might get into a frightful snit if he **heard** them being uttered.

Thus, we still have long lists of unspeakable words and unpublishable ideas, because old brain, where primitive imprints are stored, still fears that primordial thunder-god **(who appears, incidentally, on the sound track of almost every horror movie,** when the director wants to activate our deepest collective anxieties.)

Even people who think they have outgrown the thunder-god and the taboos of the Old Stone Age will find certain atavistic fears creeping up on them, in some modern works of art which deliberately violate taboos and conventional ways of thinking. Sen. Jesse Helms—who is financed by people who make a living literally poisoning us—can always make headlines by finding a new work of art which activates the dread of the Thunder God.

The same is true of the present book, so I warn you again that, if you think certain ideas and images can be dangerous to us—can literally bring down "curses from heaven" (the roars of the Giant Thing in the Sky)—this book can be extremely hazardous to your health. If you are in the censorship business, perhaps the safest course is not to read the book at all, and just issue a general condemnation of it based on your ideas about what might be found in here if you dared to read more than 5 or 10 of the eldritch and unhallowed pages that follow. Of course, condemning books you haven't read always sounds goofy to the uninitiate and ungodly; but then condemning what you know nothing about represents a long and honorable tradition among censors, who have never worried about the fact that they very often sound goofy, batty, buggy or just plain whacko to the rest of us.

After all, censorship consists chiefly of reading books that are suspected of causing degeneracy and depravity among their readers. The censor is therefore, by definition, a person constantly risking self-destruction and moral decay. What Dorian Grey-like loathsomeness must result after three or

Psychopathology Of Sex And Religion

four years of hard work as a censor staggers the imagination—the mind conjures images from *Tales from the Crypt*. But some persist in this risky profession for five years, for ten, sometimes for twenty. The total corruption that must result invokes thoughts of the lower and most excremental pits of Dante's Inferno.

One can admire the courage of those who undertake such perilous quests, but one also wonders a bit about their foolhardiness or downright masochism.

Consider: Charles Keating, who first came to public notice as leader of the National Organization for Decent Literature, spent years scrutinizing the centerfolds of **Playboy,** which he suspected of being hazardous. After intensely studying 12 of these licentious American Beauties every year, Keating was indeed corrupted. He currently stands convicted of massive junk bond swindles and embezzlements, and is accused of bribing five U.S. Senators—who were probably corrupted by the same **Playboy** pictorials, unless they had already proceeded to "the hard stuff"—**Penthouse** or **Hustler.**

(Many censors have not yet discovered the difference between these magazines. Allow me to enlighten them. The naked ladies in **Playboy** look as if they want you to make love to them. The naked ladies in **Penthouse** look as if they cannot wait any longer and have started making love to themselves. The ones in **Hustler** merely look like they are having a gynecological examination. Which of the three is more "dangerous" depends on which school of theology or mythology you embrace.)

I think it is safe to predict that almost every organized group of idiots in the country will regard this book as extremely dangerous. (If only we had some Maplethorpe illustrations we'd get a unanimous chorus of outrage from **all** the idiots in the country...) Personally, I have read the whole book and feel totally unharmed. I learned two or three "occult" secrets I didn't know before, so in that sense I was actually **enriched** by the book. (New information enriches the brain in both a metaphoric and a very literal sense. See my *Prometheus Rising* (New Falcon, 1990) on the relationship between information and wealth.) However, those who sincerely believe in the idea that a book can kill should be wary here.

This son of a bitch will seem to explode in their hands.

CHAPTER ONE

THOU SHALT NOT...

> Taboo: (1) A prohibition excluding something from use, approach, or mention because of its sacred and inviolable nature. (2) A ban or inhibition attached to something by social custom or emotional aversion. (3) A proscription devised and observed by any group for its own protection.—adj. Forbidden or excluded from use, approach, or mention: A taboo subject.

The readers of this book are warned that it contains descriptions of practices which might be considered by some horrid or shocking.

The case histories, theories and rituals presented deal primarily with the "taboo" of the uniting of sex and religion. This is often referred to in modern times as Sex Magick. We will provide the reader with an overview of the practices of Sex Magick both in ancient and in modern times. The data is by no means exhaustive nor does it provide scientific proof of the harmfulness or harmlessness of these practices. What it will show beyond a shadow of a doubt is that Sex and Religion are still practiced today as a single unit. There is no separation of the two for the Sex Magician. Modern religion and psychology have not been able to eliminate these ancient practices and in fact, according to our sources, there is an ever increasing movement to legitimize this behavior making it, if you would, a religion much like Tantra, the Eastern Tradition of Sexual Yoga. If nothing else there is more and more literature appearing on this taboo topic.

We have avoided mentioning many of the names of groups, individuals and organizations which practice these taboos. Some readers might feel that the lack of these references diminishes the credibility of this book. This is a reasonable assumption, but has been done for two very specific reasons: (1) to protect their privacy and (2) to avoid being sued.

Recently, a number of organizations which practice *religious sex* have successfully sued writers and publishers who have mistakenly confused their practices with Satanism.

Many individuals erroneously believe that Sex Magick and Satanism are one and the same. While Satanists have been known to practice Sex Magick, most Sex Magicians are not Satanists. In fact many "normal" people regularly practice Sex Magick in one form or another and do not realize it. This simple fact is considered by some religious experts to be one of the greatest dangers of Sex Magick, since they believe that the violation of such taboos can do nothing but bring evil into the world.

The "evil" nature of Sex Magick is without question not in the domain of Science. However, if we view evil as an intentional act with no redeeming value, designed to do harm, then Sex Magick cannot be lumped into that category. But if we view evil as many people might—as a violation of the laws of the Old and New Testaments—then many forms of Sex Magick might be called evil, while other forms might be considered moral and good (although these practices would not be labelled as Sex Magick by *these* practitioners). This is particularly true for those who use icons, prayers and the name of God in association with sex acts.

At the moment it would be anyone's guess if a poll were taken and Sex Magick as described by its rituals were presented as an issue whether or not the majority of those polled would consider it evil. Of course, evil determined by consensus must also take into account the nature of the people being polled. Most likely Sex Magick is evil to the born-again Christian, pathological (at best) for many psychologists trained in the 50's and 80's and merely an interesting practice for the anthropologist and the religious scholar. Like most things considered good or evil the final determination of its nature is the result of those who have the power to make the decision.

Sex Magick has been associated in the mind of the public with blood drinking, child abuse, ritual torture, cannibalism, animal and human sacrifice. Religious leaders and the media have not been innocent in the matter of encouraging the belief that Sex Magick is violent or Satanic. Modern observers have pointed out that the proliferation of the reports of heinous crimes such as serial murders, complete with elements of sexual torture, mutilation and cannibalism, have increased with the popularity of books, movies and television programs dealing with these same unsavory subjects as entertainment and "News."

The public's fascination with the details of these crimes is particularly indicative of the need to deal with the darker aspects of our own natures. We allow ourselves to experience these acts vicariously, from the safe distance of the television or motion picture screen. Unthinkable as these crimes are, we secretly identify with the perpetrator and the victim and dwell upon the perverted expressions of power and control which appear to be the underlying motivation for these acts.

Often the violent criminal projects his own need of control upon a deity who is "responsible" for his monstrous behavior. "The Devil made me do it..." may be a cliché but insanity pleas based upon claims of supernatural influence have been taken seriously by the court systems in a number of celebrated trials.

Titillating as these "satanic" projections are upon the mind of the public, they do not necessarily constitute an occult connection with the crimes. And even though many of these atrocities include elements of sexual abuse they can hardly be defined as a variety of Sex Magick.

Taboo: The Ecstasy Of Evil

Before we attempt to further examine Sex Magick it might be a good idea to first understand the meaning of the words Sex and Magick.

The word "sex" is derived from the Latin "secus" meaning to divide or separate. According to Judeo-Christian legends, upon which most of Western civilization has modeled its attitudes of good-evil, after Adam and Eve ate of the Tree of the Knowledge of Good and Evil, they became capable of discrimination. Prior to this division the first created Being was considered to be hermaphroditic, created in the exact likeness of the androgynous God, Elohim (in Hebrew, the word Elohim is a masculine plural of a feminine noun and is more accurately translated Gods). Some metaphysical and religious experts believe that Adam/Eve would have had no idea that they were separate until they ate the proverbial Apple.

In the legend of Adam and Eve the concept of shame was introduced after they ate from the Tree of Knowledge. What were Adam and Eve ashamed of? If originally they were a whole being—a perfection in the image of God—then their shame stemmed from their new state of incompleteness, separateness and difference. We can further speculate on this metaphor that each time they looked upon each other they felt the pain of their incompleteness. They felt the tension of their separateness which was ameliorated when they joined together. At the moment of ultimate Union their incompleteness was destroyed. They were ecstatic, momentarily freed from the tension and the shame of their imperfection. They were made whole.

"Magick" has been defined as *the Science and Art of causing change to occur in conformity with Will.* By this definition any willed act is a magical act. We are all magicians. We either perform our magick efficiently or inefficiently.

The primary purpose of Sex Magick is to re-unite—to put an end to division. Much of this idea is based on the belief that we merge again into One during orgasm. We lose consciousness of self and other—much like the original Adam. *Thus Sex Magick is Love under the direction of Will.* Unlike conventional sex, one of the requirements of Sex Magick is the creation of a "conflict" between the "Will" of the operator and the desire for Union. The minds of the participants are focused on the purpose of the operation and the body is "compelled" to follow. At just the right moment the "Will" is dropped and a passion beyond description ensues which "demolishes" temporarily the egos of the participants. They are now One again, like the original Adam/Eve.

It is believed by many Sex Magicians that by combining Will with Sex, the orgasm is both more intense and holy. However, what (and whose) Will this might be are two of the primary concerns surrounding the practice of Sex Magick.

Some believe that Sex Magick can be used for any number of sinister purposes from draining power from others (See Chapter Nine for an interesting example of modern "vampirism".) to demonic possession. During these times of hyper-criticalness of everything but the traditional, Sex Magick is rapidly becoming one of the most talked about taboos. What in fact makes Sex Magick a taboo?

Firstly, it has been defined as a taboo by those who have (or imagine they have) the authority. The question is why do our modern religious authorities do so? This issue will be examined throughout this book.

Secondly it is the doctrine of many religions that the "Will" of Man is in opposition to the "Will" of God. Man's sole role is that of subservience to the "Divine Laws Of God." Satan is often seen as the willfully disobedient servant of God.

Thirdly, magick in and of itself is a taboo. After all magick was the first religion; but historically the Gods of the old religion become the Devils of the new. Much of modern day magick relies on the individual and not on a priest for sole communication with the forces of the universe. Modern organized religion would see this as blasphemous competition. The war between magick and religion is not something new. The Bible makes frequent reference to sorcery, magicians and witchcraft. For example in Leviticus XX, 6: "If a man has recourse to the spirits of the dead or to magicians, to prostitute himself by following them I shall set my face against that man and outlaw him from his people."

Finally, it is the deliberate combination of religious icons, words, practices and rituals with the acts of sex which may be the very reason why Church authorities and law enforcement officials often correlate Sex Magick with idolatry and Devil worship. Does not the Second Commandment prohibit the creation of images and icons? How much greater the transgression to link a forbidden image with powerful and prohibited forces of sex?

An example might serve here. I once treated a patient who was a very successful prostitute. She attributed her financial success to the large tips she would receive from her many repeat clients. Although she had no training in techniques of Voodoo or magick she devised the following magical procedure.

To represent each of her important clients she constructed a small but simple "voodoo" doll made from coat hangers or wood and cloth. Upon these she performed improvised magical rituals to make her clients give her more money than they agreed upon. She would carry these dolls in her purse. After sex, in the privacy of the bathroom, she would take some of the genital fluids and smear them upon the heart of the doll. As she was getting ready to leave, the "enchanted" client would almost invariably hand her extra money.

While the efficacy of this procedure is no doubt questionable, it is interesting to note how naturally she developed this classic ritual of sympathetic magick, particularly since she had no conscious interest in the occult. She, like many other prostitutes I have treated, had a bag of magical and spiritual tricks. It could well be that the hardness and uncertainty of their lives pushed them into such "primitive" expressions of control.

What are some of the real dangers of such behavior if it is nothing but an acting out of wishful thinking? At this point in time Sex Magick has not become a serious threat to society, however, the issue of AIDS may make it one, although unsafe sex is unsafe sex no matter what you call it. Oral sex and the consumption of the so-called "Magick Elixir" is, of course, a concern in the AIDS matter. Another concern is the legality of such acts. According to New York's LAMBDA Legal Defense and Education Fund Inc., seventeen States still have prohibitive statutes concerning fellatio and cunnilingus between consenting adults, even married partners. This is especially notable considering the almost universal acceptance of such sexual behavior in America.

Sex Magick can be practiced without the consumption of the "Elixir," and "Sacred Talismans" can still be made and "consecrated" safely. The ramifications of the illegality of oral sex in some States are something each individual must decide for themselves. It appears that arrests are uncommon unless law enforcement officials are interested in the person for other reasons.

The reader will no doubt be aware that some of our case histories represent severe pathological states. However, to state the case that they have been caused by the practice of Sex Magick can not be made. It is well known that pathological individuals are generally attracted to fringe activities. And what factor more than religion has made sexuality a pathology?

Although there are instances where Sex Magick can heal, the real dangers of Sex Magick may lie in the fact that its practices can potentiate existing psychopathology. This issue, however, can be applied to most anything: e.g., shopping, eating, religion. The best things practitioners of the healing arts can do is to understand these practices and help patients deal with the issues brought to consciousness by the practice of Sex Magick. It is our view that practitioners will be confronted with many issues that combine religion and sex and find patients attempting to integrate them. In passing, it is interesting to note that for Jung and his followers Sex Magick would be considered neither Good nor Evil, but an expression of the Psyche attempting to integrate sexual passion with religion. Freudians, on the other hand, would see Sex Magick as regressive and blatantly pathological, particularly since they believe that religion itself is a form of mass neurosis.

It might be said that the "relapsed" state of the human soul expressed by those who regard religion as a pathology or those who regard sex as evil, is the result of our compulsive Protestant sexual morality. Like pornography, the "evil" quality associated with Sex Magick might be a result of our own prohibitions against natural human sexuality and not the cause of moral depravity. Many would claim, however, that Sex Magick is more natural and more healthy, AIDS aside, than our modern sexual expressions since it integrates God *and* Sex. For the Sex Magician, God is here and now and not off somewhere in the Universe separated by a gigantic veil from His creation.

Western culture has separated sexuality from spirit and love, creating mechanical, compulsive sexuality, adultery, pornography and sexual violence. To claim that our compulsive sexual morality is necessary to control these "demons of the soul" is confusing consequence with cause. Rape, sexual perversion and dysfunction appear to be more the result of a depraved morality than the reason to have such a morality for a protection from these "evils."

An important question concerning consenting adults must be addressed here. There are, no doubt, people who claim to be Sex Magicians who use children for their practices and force people to participate in their rites with threats of violence. However, this same claim can be made against any person or group who takes advantage of minors or uses violence to achieve their ends. Many references in Sex

Magick literature which refer to the sacrifice of babies has to do with menstrual blood or masturbation and the "waste" of semen and ovum. Historically, babies have been used as sacrifices, although significantly less than those sacrificed in wars. In reality it is less likely that Sex Magicians would use violence or violate the rights of others since, as the rituals presented herein demonstrate all participants must consent for the best results to be achieved.

I have known cases where Sex Magicians have practiced their art invoking divine names silently, using the "Elixir" to make talismans, etc. without their partner knowing. However, I have not heard of one case where any harm came to the other person which could be directly attributed to the acts of Sex Magick. There are some cases where individuals have had severe anxiety and depressive reactions after practicing Sex Magick, but in my experience this has more to do with fear of punishment and preexisting sexual pathology than with Sex Magick. After all, the Hindus as well as others have been practicing their forms of Sex Magick for thousands of years.

Many Sex Magicians believe that their art is the only way to properly escape the twin horns of pornography and compulsive sexual morality. They believe that the practice of their sacred esoteric rituals which have as their goal the re-fusing of matter and spirit can provide a means to counter-act the damage done by sex-negative religions.

The "Evil" of Sex Magick appears to simply rest on the fact that Religion and Sex in our modern Western world have been separated. "In the Beginning" Sex and Religion were one. Now they are two. The holiness has been taken out of sex, relegating it to a necessary but dangerous and evil function.

Sex Magick as a technique can be useful in helping some patients confront the split between religion and sex which many modern religions have created and, sadly enough, many mental health practitioners have helped to perpetuate.

Making "natural" sex "evil" has spawned more mental illness than almost any other single factor.

What follows is a case history where the practice of Sex Magick helped heal a severe trauma. In 1974 a young man came to me and after some months related an interesting story.

He was ten years old quietly lying in bed fantasizing about the two women living above him in the attic. They had to walk down a flight of stairs which passed through his bedroom. He was hoping that they would come down and go to the bathroom so he could peek through the keyhole and see them bathe. Finally, to his surprise one of them came down in her nightgown. He pretended he was asleep while all the time hoping that she would go to the bathroom. His excitement was building to gigantic proportions. She went into the bathroom and started running the bath water. He waited for a few moments, crawled silently out of his bed and sneaked to the bathroom door where he bent over and looked through the keyhole. His heart was beating rapidly and he began to sweat when he felt something behind him. He turned and saw his father who grabbed him by the arm and pulled him away. The boy remained silent all the time feeling the horror as it mixed with the fading pleasure he had just experienced. He was asked in a angry voice what he was doing. He replied he was looking through the keyhole to see if she was finished bathing. He continued that he had to go to the bathroom. His father pulled him down a flight of stairs into the basement where he presented him with a pan and ordered him to urinate. The boy tried but very little urine came out. The boy's mind was frozen and running wild at the same time. He continued to force himself—to make the urine "happen."

The father took the boy back upstairs to the parent's bedroom where he angrily informed the boy's mother that he was looking through the keyhole at the house border.

The mother lay silently in bed and all of sudden pulled off her covers, yelling, "... if you want to see what a women looks like—look at me. God will punish you for what you want." The boy saw the outline of her pubic hairs as he turned his head away in shame and horror. He remembered his desire to keep looking while twisting his head away. He didn't remember leaving the room nor saying anything further. What he did remember was the need not to say or do anything else. Horror, lust, passion, fear and rage had merged into one picture. He could not let his father know how much he wanted to look at his mother nor of his desire to jump into bed with her—at least to get away from the hands of his father.

As an adult my patient took an interest in Sex Magick. This interest caused him great anxiety and depression at first although he continued on with his practices. He literally had to "face the issue head on" which had caused him so much pain and agony. As a result of his continued practices he was finally able to "look." He consciously confronted the issue of his fears concerning God and Sex.

CHAPTER TWO

THE BLACK BEAUTY AND THE PRIEST

Much of my interest in Sex Magick was stimulated by a dream that a psychotic patient had in the 1970's. This dream was so striking and had such powerful consequences in her life that it has remained with me until this day.

My patient was a beautiful black woman, who suffered from severe paranoia. In her dream she was carried into a church by a young white priest. He lay down in front of the altar, lifted his black raiment under which he was naked, and she, wearing a mini-skirt and no underwear, straddled him. His penis penetrated deep inside her, and she rhythmically moved her hips in a semi-circular motion. As he ejaculated into her he called out "Jesus forgive me!" At that moment she had an orgasm unlike any she had before, whether in dream/fantasy or reality. She told me she felt that she had been completely consumed by tremendous power and love at the very moment the priest ejaculated inside her and prayed.

Within a week of the dream I was informed by her physician that she experienced a complete psychotic break and was hospitalized. The diagnosis was paranoid schizophrenia.

Her father, a deacon at their neighborhood church, had raised her to believe that a sin was "any thought, word, or deed against the law of God" (St. Augustine). It is interesting to note that many of us, to some extent, are unconsciously programmed to act as if some sort of "god" is watching us. Usually this omniscient "god" pays special attention to us when we are committing such "taboos" as masturbating, ogling our best friend's spouse, or wishing our mothers dead. Consider the simple song which has been imprinted on many a child's mind:

> You Better Watch Out! You Better Not Cry!
> You Better not pout! I'm telling you why,
> Santa Claus is Coming to Town.
> He's making a list and checking it twice,
> *He's going to find* out who's naughty and nice.
> He sees when you are sleeping. He knows when you're awake.
> He knows if you've been *bad or good,*
> So Be Good...

My patient's God just happened to be so real to her and so violently wrathful, that she was convinced that He would punish her for her lustful dream. It was her fear of punishment from God that was a "cause" of her breakdown. After a month she recovered completely and returned to her normal life. She was regarded as cured. But, in the light of what is to follow, what did that mean?

What fascinated me about the dream was its obvious content and my immediate sense that the dream signaled a nervous breakdown for my patient.

While the dream is patently pathological, it is important to ask why. By definition the violation of any taboo is pathological or sinful, and the taboo in this case was having sex with a "forbidden" person. In the dream my patient is committing a taboo act. Not only is she, a black woman, having sexual intercourse with the forbidden figure of a white priest, the sex act itself is taking place in the House of God before the Holy Altar. Thus, the taboo broken in this case is a true transgression, a violation of both location and person. The breaking of the taboo (even in a dream) so overwhelmed my patient that her mind literally broke down. Her punishment was imprisonment in a hospital.

The dream lover is also aware of breaking a great taboo. Although the priest is overjoyed in his orgasm, he asks forgiveness from Jesus for experiencing such pleasure in a house of worship and for breaking his vow of celibacy.

It is easy to see the symbolic violation of the incest taboo. My patient in the dream is having sex with a priest. A priest, of course, is commonly referred to as "father." Her father, if you recall, was a deacon. He was overly concerned with his daughters sexual purity, lecturing her often on the importance of virginity and chastity. He employed violence to enforce his beliefs and taught her that God was always watching her.

Do we dare to assume that the "dream priest," as well, commits an incestuous taboo, as he calls out the name of Jesus at orgasm? If Jesus, the Son, is inseparable from the Holy Trinity, isn't calling out the name of Jesus frighteningly close to calling out the name of God, the Father, or "Our Father" as Christians call Him when reciting "The Lord's Prayer."

The greatest orgasm is often attained during times of great risk. What could be riskier than breaking a great taboo? Criminals often speak of the thrill and intense empowerment they feel when breaking a law or social taboo. Perhaps then the greatest joy, insight, power, and yes, orgasm, is the child of those sexual acts which violate sacred, cultural, and religious taboos. William Blake, in his poem "The Garden of Love," suggested that the Church and State are the creators of taboos: "Bind with Briars our joys (as well as our power to fulfil) our desires." Was he on to something?

The greatest joy, the greatest punishment, the greatest publicity, as well as the greatest insight, comes about through violating cultural and religious taboos. But, is this last analysis true—is it only the violation of the taboo which leads to the "great" orgasm or is it something else as well? In this primitive dream is there not something of Sex Magick? Is not God and Sex unified in the same scene?

CHAPTER THREE

DAMNED IF YOU DO

Taboos throughout the ages have been devised and established by the "fathers" or "mothers" of the systems of church, state, and "normal" society. It is believed that taboos are essential in order to keep the system functioning and any act which breaks a taboo must be either criminal (sin) or pathological (illness), requiring action on part of the system to "right" the "wrong."

The most fascinating aspect of all taboos is the fundamental confusion between the content of the taboo, (e.g., don't eat pork, or don't shoot birds with yellow feathers) and the power of prohibition itself. The functional formula which makes taboos effective is that the violation of a taboo must be followed by punishment. In order for the punishment to be effective it must first be internalized by the victim, so even if he is not caught by the authorities he is apprehended and punished by his God. It is this internalization and formalism which gives a taboo its real power.

It is often thought that taboos are simply something in which only primitives believe. However, a few moments of thought will demonstrate how many taboos are believed to contain necessary prohibitions by "modern" man without one ounce of proof to substantiate them. For example, it has been said that there are 613 "Thou shalts" and "Thou shalt nots" in the Bible. Each of these is a taboo.

Probably two important questions are:
1. How does a particular taboo accomplish the goal of protecting man and society? And
2. At what costs?

The best way to answer these questions is to ask yourself: who benefits from unsubstantiated belief systems and how?

Sex Magick is the supreme attempt at unifying will power (discipline) and complete abandonment (surrender to instinct) within a religious framework. Now, why should this be taboo? Some have said that the ecstasy achieved during Sex Magick is unattainable elsewhere except perhaps through the use of drugs. Others believe that the mixing of Sex and Religion is the sure road to insanity and, after all, didn't my patient have a mental breakdown after her "Sex Magick" dream?

It is true, from our experience, that people interested in Sex Magick seem more unstable than those who are not. Is the practice of Sex Magick the cause of their instability, or is their attempt to re-unite Sex and Religion (which have been separated by a priestcraft or government) a sign of their desire for a deeper sanity? Could it be that "normal" sexuality is more crazy than it might appear?

Is there not a clue here that what might be truly pathological is the splitting off of Religion and Sex and not their union? If this were the case then we must ask ourselves why and how religion became separated from sex and how sex became separated from religion.

CHAPTER FOUR

IT'S SO HOLY
IT'S DIRTY

What goes through people's minds while they are making love to each other is usually not talked about. Isn't it ironic that some of the most creative thoughts and energies are never consciously shared, yet these thoughts are believed by the Sex Magician to be transferred to the womb.

The Sex Magician believes that the veil between the physical and the spiritual plane is transparent, while the priests of the newer religions believe the veil to be opaque. For the priest the other side is forbidden territory.

How did the priests teach their parishioners to keep their mind pure during intercourse? They didn't. Instead they taught them a form of Sex Magick which is very dangerous. Their stated objective to keep evil out of the world was actually, from the Sex Magician's point of view, the reason why evil prevailed.

Or as the prophet said:

> ...the spilling of the blood of the lamb being a ritual of the Dark Brothers, for they have sealed up the Pylon with blood, lest the Angel of Death should enter therein...the blood that they have sprinkled on their Pylon, that is a bar against the Angel of Death is the key by which he entereth in.
> (Note: the reference to the Dark Brothers is of course to the Priests.)

Taboo: The Ecstasy Of Evil

The artificially imposed taboos against Sex Magick have and will always bring about the results most unwanted by those who have instituted the taboos.

This is very similar to the issue of rape in modern society. Much of rape is the result of repression, yet more repression is always the answer to rape.

THE SELF CREATION—TABOO

Little has been said about the notion of Self Creation sometimes symbolized by the Infinity sign and other times by jokes of adolescents trying to have sex with themselves.

Very few individuals pay much attention to the fantasy or dream which reflects the archaic need to be one's own father or mother.

GODS HAVING SEX WITH MEN

In modern times it would be regarded as insane or blasphemous for Gods to make love with men. However, in more ancient times it was not uncommon for individuals to fantasize making love to Gods or Goddesses.

The mother of Alexander the Great insisted that he was not the son of Phillip, her husband, but was sired by Zeus Himself. Zeus also was the father of Hercules. Mars fathered Romulus and Remus; Vishnu appeared as an albino elephant to sire the Buddha. The mother of Arjuna, the great warrior of the Bhagavad Gita, gave birth to him and his four brothers as the result of mating with various Gods whom she could invoke with a secret mantra.

But to the Western mind, perhaps the most shocking example of religious/sexual taboo was practiced by the tribeswomen of Southern India who periodically ventured deep into the jungle to offer themselves as "wives" to the great apes. This variation of the King Kong theme was intended to achieve physical incarnations of Hanuman, the monkey god. Whether a biological possibility or not, children of these unions were allegedly raised in the Temple and worshipped as divine.

PATIENTS HAVING SEX WITH DOCTOR—GODS

The case for patient and doctor sexual encounters representing aspects of Sex Magick rites can not be made conclusively. Obviously, there are few physicians or other doctors who have sex with patients and claim they are practicing Sex Magick. The fact that the patient is making love to a "God" or "Goddess" image can argue for some aspects of this illegal relationship having some qualities of the theory of Sex Magick. In fact certain ancient and some modern groups of Sex Magicians hold that if a "higher" person performs Sex Magick with a "lower" less evolved person the latter will be elevated. However, it is cautioned that the reverse might take place, unless the Magician can exert supreme control over the operation.

While I was in practice I heard of many cases of doctors having sexual relations with patients, all of which had the component of the patient "receiving power" by making love to the Mana person. There was, for many patients, a temporary relief from all symptoms. What the doctor receives is no doubt worship, some safety from ridicule and of course "easy" sex. For the moment he was in charge, although this position could reverse itself quite rapidly. Perhaps the ideas of Power and "God" images associated with sex is enough to lump these illegal asymmetrical relations into the category of Sex Magick. I for one do not think so. Sex Magick not only deals with the power between people, but with the power of the Universe. Many Sex Magicians speak of their art as always containing the "Other"—God. Also most competent and ethical Sex Magicians practice their art in the service of a principle or a specific goal.

CHAPTER FIVE

SEX AND RELIGION

Of course, copulation with gods and demons has not always been viewed as "evil." As mentioned earlier Leda is seen to be ravished by Zeus who comes in the form of a white swan. This intercourse is often thought of as violent, powerful and brutal. The communion of God with a mortal is not passive, but fiery and energetic, making it more like what we call Western Sex Magick and unlike Eastern Tantric practices which are often thought of as more genteel. This myth has been seen as the forerunner of the immaculate conception of the modern God, Gentle Jesus.

The experience of Saint Teresa of Avila (circa 1552) is perhaps the most famous example in Western culture of the ecstasy of the fiery, divine intercourse. Idealized in marble by the master sculptor Bernini, the famous vision has held generations of the devout in awe. Saint Teresa, a capable and prolific writer described an angel, armed with a long golden spear with a "fiery tip" who repeatedly:

> "plunged it into my deepest inward. When he drew it out, I thought my entrails would be drawn out too, and when he left me I glowed in the hot fire of love for God. The pain was so strong that I screamed aloud but simultaneously I felt such an infinite sweetness that I wished the pain to last forever. It was the sweetest caressing of the soul by God."

Taboo: The Ecstasy Of Evil

The Pentecostal image is closer to the fiery quality of Leda and the Swan than to the image of Jesus' conception. Here a fiery dove or bird figure comes down from "heaven" and impregnates the Apostles with the Holy Spirit. Consider that Angels are often depicted with Swan-like white feathery wings. Long ago, in matriarchal cultures, it was a commonly accepted religious practice for ordinary men to be chosen for the privilege of copulating with a sacred prostitute, a woman who was the true embodiment of the Goddess. In some modern sex cults this woman is referred to as the Whore of Babalon—an evil image according to modern Christianity.

According to Blake, the Christian world sees Good as Passive and Energy as Evil. ("The Meek Shall Inherit The Earth"). Thus power and will is turned into gentleness and love. This is the transformation of energetic willful passionate sex into sex under the guidance of Christ. If this is so then Sex Magick, which requires full consciousness and action, is evil on many counts. It is the conscious control of life and creation, it is willful and usurps the power of the Sacred Authority of God as administered by Jesus and his Church.

As humans we may accept the animal nature of our bodies, even those parts of our bodies which are sometimes referred to as "dirty." As the poet Yeats pointed out "Love pitched his mansion in the place of excrement." And didn't a well known Catholic saint state that we are born between urine and feces? His statement however, was to attest to the dirty quality of the sexual apparatus. Godliness, most of us have been taught, is next to cleanliness. And although many religions teach that "God is everywhere," He seems to be conspicuously absent below the "belt." It is certainly taboo to think of God meandering about in urine and fecal matter. But the disassociation of religion from sex on the basis that the penis and vagina have dual functions as channels for the elimination of body wastes, and the creation of life can be a plausible explanation. Thus, it might be said that modern religion couldn't regard sex or the sexual organs as a worthy religious "house" on two points, (1) "image" making, and (2) the association of God with purity.

For a moment contemplate the number of men and women around the world shouting out the various names of Gods at the instant of orgasm. Imagine a 30 year old Catholic lawyer making love to his girlfriend under a crucifix which was blessed by the Pope. Certain fundamentalist Christians are taught that sex is OK as long as one keeps Jesus in his or her mind during the act.

And what about the countless expectant mothers and fathers who pray to Mary or Jesus or God or the Holy Spirit during the sexual act for a much desired boy, or girl. Does not such a prayer incorporate Desire, Love, Will, and God in the same sexual act?

Picture the Orthodox Jew anxiously waiting for Sabbath in order to have his most holy and joyous sex.

What about the often quoted statistic that most sex takes place on Sunday, the same day of Christian worship? The religious Jew also has many rituals surrounding sex. These include cleansing baths which "assure" that the blood of menstruation is washed away so the "blood" taboo is not violated. Remember, "the blood is the life" and the maxim of the Sex Magician is "There is no part of me that is not of the Gods."

Can it be that what we regard as normal and healthy sex is truly pathological and Sex Magick the healthier?

CHAPTER SIX

WHEN RELIGION WAS SEX

> The unseen Power whose eye Forever doth accompany mankind Hath looked on no religion scornfully That mankind did ever find.
>
> Matthew Arnold

If we take a look at the roots of religion, we find that ritualistic Sex, or Sex Magick, was the favorite religion of early man. Sex was exalted as a gift of the Gods and as the appropriate form of worship for many people's favorite deities.

Ritualized sexual activity often characterized the worship of Gods associated with the creation of the world, agricultural success and abundance, as well as love and fertility generally. In fact, the word "Lust," in Old German, means "religious joy."

The countless Spring and Summer agricultural festivals of pre-Christian Europe were characterized by all manner of overt acts of ritualized sex. These were not merely isolated instances of accidental excesses, but the central theme of the rites themselves.

Modern students may wish to dismiss such ceremonies as primitive expressions of homeopathic or sympathetic magic designed not for religious purposes or personal spiritual expression but just to make the crops or trees grow. The point must be made, however, that the leaf-covered Green Man and the Maiden adorned with flowers could not help but undergo a profound transcendent spiritual metamorphosis as their personal gender identities became unified with the universal male/female nature of the plants whose fecundity meant life or death to their people.

Long before it became popular to believe that suffering and submission were the roads to a happy life and after life, man sought to communicate with the Intelligence of the Planet, or as Dylan Thomas so beautifully put it "The force which through the green fuse drives the flower." It was our utmost desire to meld our wills with the Big Will of the Planetary Intelligence. This striving for connection with the Divine Will was born from our feelings of insufficiency and smallness. We feared our insignificance; it seemed that our inventions and art mattered not to the Power which pushed life along. It was this terrible feeling of insignificance, of smallness, that made Conrad's Kurtz cry out "The Horror! The Horror!" while dying in the midst of jungle and warfare.

Perhaps it was the Will of the Planet to constantly remind us of our weakness in order to provoke us to strive for power and life itself thereby furthering its relatively slow evolutionary plan. Or perhaps the human quest for power is the trait which has helped our species survive in a Darwinian world. Whatever our philosophical bent, history tells us that early religion aimed to connect man with the power source of the planet so he might plug in, stop swimming upstream, and gain the potential power to fulfill his desires.

Friedrich Nietzsche thought that the **Will to Power** was the driving force behind all life and all movement. Most of us are taught that power is something only selfish, greedy, mean people strive for. To Will to Power is simply the need to fill up as much space as one can with oneself–and what better way to do it than with sex?

Most modern religions do not increase our potential powers, but take away the seed of power (which is the birthright of every human being) by force and coercion.

The author Barbara Walker tells us that the word "religion" is derived from the Latin "religio," meaning to re-link. The Sanskrit term for religion is yoga (the root of the English word "yoke") and also means to join. The original purpose of religion was to bind man with the Earth. This Sacred Union was typically described as Divine Love between man and woman and God and Goddess.

From Aeschylus, for instance, we see the semen of the Sky from the Titan Uranus, penetrating the Earth Goddess Gaia resulting in the birth of the Gods and every living thing including mortals.

Before life was demoted to the position of a mere springboard to the hereafter, Man demanded action from his Gods. They insisted on results, here and now; if the God did not give results He was fired. Our ancestors had daily to deal with insuring fertility of crops, animals and themselves, healing and protection from enemies. Even the ancient Hebrews looked on God as an earth-results oriented Deity. A religion which didn't demonstrate its effectiveness was discarded. Our ancestors would have applauded Carlyle when he wrote that without results religion is "at best...an anxious wish; a great Perhaps."

Much of early religion with its emphasis on "cause and effect" was behaving as if it were an empirical science. Its practitioners, perhaps, were semi-existentialists relying more on their senses and actions than on prayer, knowing a "truth" by what they experienced, heard or saw. The desire for results and the courage to experiment and test "theories" is at the core of the first religion, sometimes called Magick. One famous modern day magician states it this way: "Our method is Science. Our aim is Religion."

Early man developed many action oriented methods for the purpose of attaining connection with the Divine. Many of these methods entailed the temporary dissolution or "death" of our small mechanical self. By the death of our small selves, our "True Will," (or to paraphrase Dylan Thomas, *the Force Which Through the Monkey Drives the Man*) was exposed. Stripped of our mechanical Monkey Suit, we connected, combined, and communed with the Force Which Drives The Flower, as well as the Fish, The Wind, The Fire,

Taboo: The Ecstasy Of Evil

The Planet, The Universe, The Gods. Then, like magic, the rain came, or we knew intuitively where to go and find a clear stream, or the hickory branch told us where to dig for water.

Some wise men and women found that prolonged and frenzied dancing, enthusiastic drumming, intoxication and, especially ecstatic lovemaking worked to dissolve our small wills (and in a much more joyful and exuberant manner than the ascetic methods of fasting, and suffering which later became popular with the advent of the modern religion Christianity.)

D.H. Lawrence, a fairly modern writer who worked towards stripping sex of its "bad reputation," said "in pure, fierce, passion of sensuality I am burned into essentiality." The essentiality which Lawrence speaks of is the "True Will" which is at once our own, yet also the Will of Everything. A Hermetic philosopher described this experience as an encounter with God whose "center is everywhere and circumference nowhere found."

The Dionysians, one of the most popular of the Sex-centric religions, practiced the art of excess to "remove" the small will and join with the Universe. "Enough! or Too Much!" was their cry; prudence was a quality which their gods did not sanctify. One could not know one's power or one's own limits, until those limits were tried. It seems the members of these Sex-centric religions successfully achieved some desired results from their practices, for the cults of Dionysius and other sex-loving Gods became as popular as Coca-Cola in the 1920s (before the cocaine was removed).

Many Sex-centric religions saw the Planetary Intelligence as a fertility Goddess—a Life giver. Our ancestors, like ourselves, explained their world through metaphor. But man of old, not having invented the more "scientific" metaphors of our times, explained that there was a grand and mighty penis above the sky which would ejaculate the "seed" of god, or rain. Some linguistic scholars claim that the god-names of Zeus and Yahweh were both derived from a

Sumerian word meaning "juice of fecundity" or "seed of life." The earth was seen as a womb, containing the multiple "ova" of the goddess. Hence the creation of a sky "father" and an earth "mother." (Note: the heaven of our pre-Christian relatives is not to be confused with the Christian Heaven. It was simply the part of the cosmos which surrounded the earth—the "father.")

The earliest sex rituals were intended to invoke the fertility god/desses and influence them to give of their bounty. It was believed that whatever acts were performed by an individual or tribe would be imitated by the god/desses—a turnabout of the Hermetic aphorism, "as above, so below." The Sex Magicians counted on the voyeuristic tendencies of the sky "father" and earth "mother." Some of them believed that the stronger the orgasms achieved by the priests and priestesses below, the better chance that the god/desses would "hear" them and be aroused enough to make love, spew seeds, and bless the soil with fecundity. If the god/desses were not seduced to sexual embrace by the screams of their earthly counterparts, no rain would fall, the earth would be barren and the people would die.

Later, when man invented a more efficient and reliable irrigation system and was no longer dependent on the ejaculation of rain by the sky "father," the function and purpose of the sexual ritual changed. It evolved from a technique for the survival of the tribe into a method for the empowerment of the shaman as well as the individual.

Certain disciplined individuals discovered that the more they practiced tuning into the Divine Will, the more conscious they became of their true wills, and the more individual power they attained. It was as if their small weak monkey minds were gradually melting away. Their true will, their superhumanness, was being released. Some of these hard-working individuals used their new "powers" to manipulate energy. Some of these early energy technicians or artists called themselves Magicians. Others called themselves the Sons of God, or Prophets, the Blessed Ones.

Their art consisted of using the force of their Wills to consciously create physical and psychical change, usually called miracles by the ignorant. Some magicians healed the sick and fed the hungry. Some turned staffs into serpents, some caused madness. All of these *energy artists* worked hard at their craft. Many conceived new worlds or even universes, and these concepts were written down by their disciples, who, in turn, filtered the life and works of their masters in accordance with their own reality tunnels and linguistic maps. Many of the writings based on the lives, imaginations and events caused by these Artists are extant in the form of religious scriptures. Many theologians are still arguing about what these scriptures really mean, while others know and still continue to practice their ancient art.

The energy artist or Sex Magician aimed to burn away his conditioned self and contact his True Will for the purpose of finding his place and purpose in the scheme of things. Sex Magick as understood by modern practitioners is, in a sense, exactly opposite in underlying theory to the ritualized sex of the primitives who confused the "metaphor" with the "referent". Sex Magicians use metaphor as did our ancestors, but their use of the power of metaphor actually *becomes a part of* a "new referent" (if we assume that the final result of the magick is not to make the crops grow but the conscious participation in a transcendent universal process).

In this sense the practices of Sex Magick can be seen as devices leading to the re-birth or twice born experience often referred to by modern day evangelical Christians. In the Holy Bible it is written that "Except a man be born of water and of the spirit, he cannot enter into the kingdom of God." (John III,.5). It is impossible to be born again unless one dies. Let us infer, for a moment, that a "little death" occurs at the point of orgasm. A spiritual rebirth, then, might be in the process of dying consciously and willfully, as well as awakening consciously and willfully. That is, after one "suffers", through discipline, the little death of orgasm, one becomes conscious of completely letting go and is consciously "reborn" of water (sexual fluids) and through the God invoked during orgasm. Thus, the formula is of "spirit" and "water". No doubt the modern Christian can and will take offense to the association of Sex Magick with the formula of rebirth. He would complain that Sex and God are separate and one can not be known through the other. Secondly, he would assume that the Will of the Magician is not the Will of God.

After the rise of Christianity, the pursuit of power and the use of will came to be seen as immoral, evil, bad, or sinful. So the Art of Magic and the Will to Power were repressed and became the domain of the Devil.

The Church began to systematically destroy all elements of the old religious forms and to crush its proponents. In spite of this, the great secrets of the ancient arts were maintained. In the face of violent repression they assumed innumerable masks which veiled the teachings in words and art, signs and symbols intelligible only to initiates. They even assumed the forms of the Church itself and of its Holy Knights doing *battle* to secure Her *Holy Land.*

The military and religious order of the Knights Templar, thought by some to be Sons of Satan, have a illuminating and romantic history. Some conspiracy buffs maintain that the Knights Templar are the Secret Illuminati, existing even today, who control world events and economies through their massive wealth and magic powers. However, from the point of view of this book the interest in the Knights Templar is with their alleged involvement with Sex Magick and blasphemous crimes against God and His Church (see Chapter 21).

CHAPTER SEVEN

SEX AMONG THE PUFFERS

> In the Green Lion's bed the sun and moon are born; they are married and beget a king; the king feeds on the lion's blood, which is the kings father and mother, who are at the same time his brother and sister. I fear I betray the secret, which I promised my master to conceal in dark speech from every one who does not know how to rule the philosophers fire.
>
> from Heckethorn's
> Secret Societies of All Ages & Countries, 1896

During the Middle Ages and Renaissance periods, a group of magicians called Alchemists flourished. Sometimes derogatorily called puffers, they used their breath as billows to maintain a steady heat in their furnaces. Alchemists were seen by the public as insane men who wasted away their lives attempting to change lead into gold or find an "elixir" of immortality. Some experts believe that the "alchemical gold" was not a metal at all, but a metaphor for the Soul or True Will of the alchemist. If the Soul or Will was not hardened and cultivated during the lifetime of the alchemist, the body would fall away at death and the monkey personality would simply dissolve into the Æther. The Buddhist Diamond Sutra and the Gurdjieffian system are similar in their suggestion that the immortal soul of an individual is not a given, but something that the individual must create for himself by his own efforts.

Through the conscious burning away of the monkey self in the fire or forge of sexual passion and discipline, the alchemist connected with his True Will.

> Thou shalt separate the earth from the fire, the ethereal from the gross, gently, but with great industry.
> It ascends from earth to heaven and again it comes down from heaven to earth, and it is invested with the potency of superior and inferior things.
> Thou wilt possess by this means the glory of the whole world, and all darkness will depart from thee.
> It is the strong power of every power, for it will overcome all things subtle and penetrate all things solid.
> It is thus that the world was created.
>
> E. Levi
> Mysteries of Magic 1896

Further practice of special sexual techniques was thought to strengthen the individual's Will, calcifying it so that it would keep its form after the death of the physical body. (An added attraction to this Work was that the alchemist who achieved this "apotheosis" was also said to attain the power to fulfill the more material desire of transmuting lead into gold.) This "Philosopher's Stone" also had its physical and biological correspondence in the body of the Alchemist himself.

> This stone, say the masters must not be exposed to the air, nor to the glances of the profane; it must be kept concealed and preserved with care in the most secret place of the owner's laboratory, and the key of that place must be always carried about the person...The wise man more readily preserves it in its natural envelopes which the Kabbalists call skins.
>
> E. Levi (*op. cit.*)

If the way to Godhood demanded hard work on the part of the individual and could not be attained vicariously as modern Christianity promises, why weren't the alchemical sexual practices more popular in the West? The obvious reason is that Sex Magicians, priests and priestesses would have been burned as heretics by the Papal judicial system. The Church would lose its power and its followers if the people took responsibility for their own souls and (God forbid) realized their own divine True Wills. From the view point of the Church, the transfiguration of religious subjects from mechanical monkeys into living, loving, joyful humans is considered dangerous to decency, order and the well being of commerce.

In summary, to the early agricultural tribes, to the Dionysians, to the Eastern Tantrics, and to the Alchemists, the practice of conscious sexuality or Sex Magick was not just a part of their religion—SEX WAS RELIGION in the purest sense. Sex is now disassociated from religious purity, to the point that to combine the two in the modern Western world is thought by the masses to be Satanic.

Please pay special attention to The Mass of the Holy Ghost in Chapter Twenty Six, Sexual Alchemy

CHAPTER EIGHT

THE DEVIL YOU SAY

And the serpent was cunning above every animal of the field which Jehovah God had made.
Genesis III, 1.

The great dragon, the primeval serpent, known as the devil or Satan, who had deceived all the world, was hurled down to the earth and his angels were hurled down with him.
Revelation XII, 9

Therefore, be wise as serpents, and harmless as doves.
Matthew X, 16

The Devil is, historically, the God of any people that one personally dislikes...This serpent, Satan, is not the enemy of Man, but He who bade "Know Thyself!" and taught Initiation. He is "The Devil" of the Book of Thoth, and His emblem is Baphomet, the Androgyne who is the hieroglyph of arcane perfection...He is Man made God, exalted, eager; he has come consciously to his full stature and is ready to set out on his journey to redeem the world. But he may not appear in this true form; the Vision of Pan would drive men mad with fear. He must conceal himself in his original guise.
Aleister Crowley
Magick In Theory and Practice (Magickal Childe Publishing 1991)

Somewhere along the historical line, sex became associated with sin. Eve was tempted by a serpent (a phallic power symbol). It is interesting to note that the serpent has always been a symbol of power rather than a symbol of either good or evil in and of itself. Its ability to shed its skin makes it an especially appropriate symbol of eternal life. While snakes generally have a bad name even in our modern times, we might remember that Moses used serpents to prove that he was a more powerful magician than the Pharaoh's magicians. (Ex VIII, 1 to 12) "And the Lord spake to Moses...take thy rod and cast it before Pharaoh and it shall become a serpent." Moses' supreme power was illustrated as his serpents swallowed the serpents of the Pharaoh's top magicians. So in that story, the serpent aided Moses in his task of liberating his people. Also, Qabalistically the number representative of the Messiah (Mshich) and the serpent (Nchsh) is the same number of the Hebraically (358). Some modern scholars have pointed out that the Hebraic numerical equivalent of (ShM YHShVH) "Name Jesus" is in fact the number of the Beast "666." Nevertheless, this fact, which horrifies some people, is easily verifiable by anyone who knows the numerical equivalents of the Hebrew alphabet.

Also, we must not forget that our central nervous system, spine and brain make us a variety of "snakes with limbs," complete with a very important reptilian brain. Isn't it odd that the serpent of Genesis was cursed to "crawl on your belly?" How did he get around before that?

There is, of course, great controversy as to whether the Fall into duality or division was a fortunate or unfortunate development. One modern theologian holds that the pain of division is nothing when compared to the joy of dissolution that accompanies divine union.

But how was it that sex became associated with sin? We might assume that sex is the most God-like attribute of man since sex makes man identical to God in his ability to create human beings. "And the Lord said behold, the man is become as one of Us to know good and evil...And Adam begat a son in his own likeness, after his image." Note that the same words are used to describe Adam's reproductive action as were used to describe the generative action of God. And just who was God talking to when he spoke? Who are the "Us"? The royal we? His companions, the other gods? (Maybe that's why he became so jealous later. Incidentally, the One God's fierce jealousy proves the Reality, at least in that God's mind, of other gods. One cannot, of course, be jealous of illusory or fake gods, and one cannot, unless suffering from schizophrenia or multiple personalities, be jealous of oneself.)

But sex itself wasn't vilified as sinful until St. Paul. The Old Testament records begetting going on everywhere. Multiple wives were in and babies were being born abundantly in a major effort to populate the Earth. Nor did there seem to be an unwholesome preoccupation with virtue.

> When the Lord spake at the first by Hosea, the Lord said unto Hosea, Go, take unto thee a wife of whoredom and children of whoredom for the land doth commit great whoredom, departing from the Lord. So he went and took Goher the daughter of Diblaim; and she conceived and bare him a son.
>
> Hosea I, 2 and 3

It was the lack of fertility that was the work of the devil in the minds of the Jews. Barren women were seen as accursed. The Hebrew word for widow originally meant wasted womb. Sex was, and is, a sacrament to the Orthodox Jews. Friday nights, when Sabbath officially begins is reserved for sexual intercourse between man and wife with Jehovah's blessing. In fact in this ancient religion it is the husband's duty to satisfy his wife. But something must have happened along the way of history which got man thinking that the road to Heaven meant "saying no to sexual joy". Jesus, the Saviour for the modern Western world is said to have been born of an immaculate conception. Immaculate meaning clean; Mary, the mother of Jesus, was a virgin, untarnished by sexual intercourse as the myth goes. Jesus was born without the sperm of Joseph, Mary's husband and without penetration of a penis. Now this is in direct disobedience to the Jewish law of that time. Intercourse was a must for married couples. From this point of view Joseph and Mary were a heretical couple.

Perhaps the immaculate conception metaphor has been misunderstood. Perhaps the idea was to show that Mary was impregnated by the sperm of God, Jesus' father, similar to the Greek myth of Leda and the Swan. The word Parthenogenesis stems from the Greek and signifies "birth from a virgin." (Science has enabled this to occur now in amphibians and some lower mammals.) Or perhaps Mary and Joseph were performing a ritual of Sex Magick, similar to those performed today, whereby, through meditative techniques the man and woman are actually transmuted into God and Goddess prior to and during the sex act. In that case, the fruit of Mary's womb would be a magickal child, or a true son of God and Goddess.

If we look at early Judeo/Christian writings, we discover that sinful sex had to do with the wasting of holy sperm, a blasphemy against the Fertility and War God who was sometimes associated with the liquid. This same principle can be seen in our modern times if we look at the Catholic strictures against the use of the Pill or birth control. The modern Catholic's hatred of contraceptives has little to do with morals and a lot to do with the ancient idea that the wasting of seed is a sin.

CHAPTER NINE

THE VAMPIRE

If the act of wasting one's own semen is a sin, then how much greater the transgression of one who steals it from another for nourishment?

"Vampires are real." They are very common. Anyone who consciously or unconsciously feeds themselves on your energy is a "vampire." Be honest with yourself. How many people do you know who leave you feeling "drained" of energy—who make you tired even when you see them coming. Many people, especially young adults, feel that way about one or both of their parents. One of my patients once said of her mother, "I sucked her milk for seven months and she's been sucking my blood ever since!"

Does this mean your mother is a "vampire?" Perhaps. But she certainly doesn't consider herself one. There are those who do—who feel they cannot live without the energy they get from others—who consciously attach themselves to their victims and drain them of their vitality. Some go so far as to weaken them to unconsciousness and suck their breath or drink their blood. Others vampirize their victim's semen during sex.

Note: This section should not in anyway be interpreted as a condemnation of gay sexual practices magical or otherwise. The "experiment" below is entirely coincidental to the sexual orientation of the author of the letter.

The remarkable letter below was sent to us as the result of the publication of the two books, *Enochian Sex Magick* and *The Way of the Secret Lover* (Hyatt & DuQuette, New Falcon Publications 1991). The writer characterized himself as a "Black Magician" and a "Vampire". We have withheld his name at his request.

Dear Dr. Hyatt and Mr. DuQuette,

I have just completed reading your two works, *Enochian Sex Magick* and *The Way of the Secret Lover*. I enjoyed them very much and complement you not only for your intelligent grasp of the subject (of which I consider myself a self-educated expert) but also for the courage it obviously took to deal with such subjects in print. (As I'm sure you both know, most occultists and New-Agers are such sex-negative prigs.)

I was a bit disappointed that you did not delve deeply into aspects of Gay Sex Magick—but perhaps in some future work. In the meantime I thought I'd share with you how I became a Vampire.

About ten years ago, before the AIDS epidemic put a damper on things, I used to go to a bath house every other weekend or so. As I'm sure you know, a bathhouse is a sex club that has its origins in the roman baths of the Emperor Caracalla where much the same behavior took place, and evolved through the so-called Turkish baths of the last century.

At any rate, I had been living in California for a year or so, as a grateful expatriate from the Midwest, and had been seriously practicing ceremonial magic for all of that time. I had read the account by Aleister Crowley in *Magick In Theory and Practice* regarding his alleged encounter with a "vampire." His allusions to the sexual nature of this particular kind of vampirism were very clear. He asserted that vampirism can be accomplished by means of passive oral sex. Bluntly, letting someone ejaculate in your mouth (without yourself having an orgasm) while using mental power to draw the partner's vital energy into your system. (This is something that years later I learned was a technique of left-hand Tantra, as well as Taoist Alchemy.) I rented a small room in the club, equipped with a bed and other amenities, and after a while met an attractive young blond man of about my own age. We went to my room and lay down on the bed in a *soixante-neuf* position, my penis in his mouth and his in mine. Somewhere in the middle of this fun I remembered what I had read and decided to perform an experiment in the above-mentioned kind of "psychic vampirism" to see if anything happened. So I resisted having an orgasm and allowed him to ejaculate in my mouth, while declining to return the compliment. At the moment of his orgasm, I mentally visualized vital energy in the form of white light leaving his body and entering mine via his penis. I felt no different. Thinking that the only thing I accomplished was robbing myself of a good orgasm, we got up, I toweled him off and watched him leave the room. Seconds later, I heard a loud thud outside my door, opened it, and saw my former partner laying flat-out on the floor with a confused look on his face. He told me that he felt dizzy suddenly and just collapsed from weakness. I asked him if he had been taking drugs (prevalent in that place) and he said "no".

I am sure you gentlemen are probably saying there are other explanations, but his collapse in conjunction with my experiment made me think that my first experiment in sex-magick was successful in an imperfect way. That is, I succeeded in depleting him of vital energy, but was too ignorant at the time to know how to absorb or make use of it. I am more skilled now.

CHAPTER TEN

INCUBI AND SUCCUBI
DEMONIC SEXUAL VIOLATION

> Because the incubus demon is able to steal the semen of an innocent youth in nocturnal emissions and pour it into the womb of a woman she is able by this semen to conceive an offspring whose father is not the demon incubus but the man whose semen impregnated her...Therefore it seems that a man is able without a miracle to be at one and the same time both a virgin and a father.
>
> Thomas Aquinas
> Quaestiones Quodlibetales

The fear of the loss of semen is also thought to be associated with the ancient idea that female spirit forces called Succubi are draining men (against their will) of their sperm. This is sometimes thought to be the forerunner of our modern vampire myths. The Romantic Poet Keats popularized the idea in his poem *La Belle Dame Sans Merci*. Females, as well, were known to copulate with male spiritual entities called Incubi, and many so called witches were burned by the inquisition, having been accused of intercourse with the devil or his demons.

Below is an excerpt from the journal of a 43 year old man who I was counseling through a particularly difficult divorce. I think it is a particularly revealing narrative and especially pertinent to the subject of the Incubus and Succubus—those phantoms that disguise themselves in the image of mortal lovers to seduce us in our sleep.

She stood by the bed looking more radiant and lovely than I had ever seen her. How long had it been? High School? This morning? Maybe at work? A long time, but no time at all. She hadn't changed—I think. But her eyes were so penetrating, so inviting I couldn't think. I was unaware of everything in the world but her. She spoke. I'm not sure what she said, but I immediately understood it to be a request, a lewd and urgent demand that I immediately have sex with her.
I thought, this can't be. Where is Barbara? Is she here? She'll find out! It doesn't matter.
I don't know how or when we became naked but she laid down on her back and pulled me on top of her. Her hand pulled frantically upon my penis. I had never been so sexually excited. It felt as though my entire body had become an erection. I tingled with fire not only from my groin but the back of my neck, my heart and the pit of my stomach. My whole body thrilled like in dreams of flying. She tugged and stroked and squeezed at what seemed my very soul.
We kissed, and her mouth was wet and sweet. She opened it wider and wider and I plunged my tongue deep down her throat until I became uncomfortably conscious of her teeth like a cold ring of wet ivory around my tongue. Suddenly I was distracted by what seemed a hardness in the area between her legs where I was desperately thrusting my penis.
All I could think of now was how much I wanted to penetrate her but it felt as though there was something between us—a

membrane of cloth or rubber I thought. Each thrust became more painful than the last.

I reached my hand down so I could guide myself into her when I realized there was nothing there, no vagina, no opening to penetrate. She was totally smooth!

Smooth or not I would die if I couldn't achieve release. "I'll look into her face and burst as she consumes me with her eyes", I thought. But as I glanced back up into her face and thrust my hands into her hair, great clumps of it came off in my hands in sticky, dirty mats that clung to my face, my mouth, my tongue. I began to gag, then suffocate.

Her face that had been so beautiful only an instant before had become a monstrous and skeletal shell of a sexless creature of indescribable horror. It was changing both in form and color—almost like it could not hold itself together. The face of an insect one instant and a reptile the next. From its mouth spat a litany of obscenities which it repeated like a mantra as I was pulled closer and closer to its stinking breath. Revolted and nauseated, I recoiled from it and tried to break free from its embrace.

As I twisted and squirmed I felt myself ejaculating into what seemed like mid air. I say ejaculate but unlike any I have ever experienced for there was no ecstasy no relief or satisfaction, only terror and an intense frustration similar to a suppressed sneeze only infinitely more painful and unrewarding. I was startled to hear myself moan in pain and I began to become aware that I was waking up. It was a dream. I was more embarrassed than relieved. I took one more

> glance at this creature that violated me only to realize that I was staring at my own blood-stained pillow, I had bitten my own tongue and my chin and neck were covered in blood and I realized my stomach and legs were cold and wet with my own semen.

Experiences such as this are not uncommon. Men and women of all ages are subject to periodic nocturnal "encounters" and few people can truthfully say that they have never had a "wet dream". But are Incubi and Succubi simply the subconscious imaginary mechanism which triggers "wet dreams"? Most of the world's major religions and many Sex Magicians say "no" although they disagree radically upon definition and moral implications.

It is particularly interesting to note that many of the elements of the above experience parallel countless medieval descriptions of Incubus and Succubus encounters.

What are Incubi and Succubi? Or, perhaps a more practical question, what do people think they are?

Rabbinical theories are countless, but one in particular was enthusiastically accepted by Christian demonologists of the First and Second Centuries A.D.—that the demons are Fallen Angels. This theory crystalized in the medieval mind and is the predominate influence upon the modern church as well.

Genesis VI tells us that "the sons of God," looking at the "daughters of men," saw they were pleasing, so they "married as many as they chose." These unions produced the Nephilim, Giants who in their turn mated with mortal women.

There is disagreement about the identity of the sons of God and the daughters of men. Some early Church Fathers maintained that they were the offspring of Abel and Cain, respectively. (Some UFO enthusiasts maintain that the "sons of God" are actually extraterrestrials who mated with human or ape females to facilitate the mutation of humanity.)

The more popular view, however, held that the sons of God were the angels that fell with Lucifer after the war in heaven and the daughters of men were just that—mortal females.

These unions are held responsible for the creation of monsters and the proliferation of evil. These evil "children" are sometimes flesh and blood mortals (albeit with black hearts and evil souls), or sometimes purely spiritual beings, possessed of no body. They are non-corporeal personifications of lust, greed, murder and hate.

Because they are half-human, they are possessed with a number of mortal qualities and needs. They require nourishment and those elements necessary for the life and perpetuation of the human race; blood, semen and, in the case of Incubi, a mortal womb in which to gestate their monstrous offspring.

Roaming the night like great spectral "hunting parties" Incubi and Succubi, attracted by the "unclean" thoughts of sleeping men and women, enter their dreams disguised as human dream lovers. Their object: the blood and semen of the man and the blood, ova and womb of the woman.

All this may seem silly, superstitious and absurd to the modern mind, but really, no more ridiculous than any other article of faith.

But we cannot hold the Judeo-Christian attitude exclusively responsible for these theories. Hindu occultism maintains similar views and holds that the human imagination is a powerful generator of a form of non-corporeal sperm, simply when stimulated by thoughts of lust and erotic fantasies. Incubi and Succubi are said to be created by these "ejaculations" of the imagination.

There are many tales of men being molested by Succubi, but it should be pointed out that the great majority of ancient reports concern women being violated by Incubi who were identified in some cases as the Devil himself. It is argued by modern experts that the incidences of Incubus/Succubus encounters most likely occur evenly between men and women, but because of various cultural and social/religious reasons, especially in medieval Europe, only the experiences of women ended up being reported. There is a great deal of circumstantial evidence to support this theory.

Consistent in the vast majority of reports by women of the medieval period, is that the "lover" is a black man or a large dark humanoid animal, (many times a goat) possessing a large serpentine penis often without scrotum or testicles (or more than one penis) which seemed to move with a life of its own. Some descriptions offered during the witch trials of the Sixteenth Century tell of the bifurcated penis of the Unholy One with which he simultaneously masturbated and penetrated his partner. Sometimes a third prong was employed in the mouth or rectum of his victim. Very often penetration was extremely painful and resulted in much vaginal injury and bleeding. Also, almost without exception, the ejaculated sperm was reported to be ice-cold.

Now let us turn our attention back to the experience of my patient. For it is very similar to classic Succubi reports.

First let us examine what parts of the experience differentiate it from a routine "dream."

It starts much like a normal dream with the dreamer already involved in a situation and totally unaware that he is dreaming. He recognizes an old lover or an individual with whom he has fantasized a sexual relation. There is confusion at first, but it is overcome by the passion of the moment.

Conscious elements try to exert themselves but are also overcome. We recall that my patient was briefly concerned that his wife would discover this indiscretion. In classical accounts we find similar concerns, often relating to parents or the Priest.

Secondly, we read the most significant statement of all indicating that the encounter is perhaps more than a common dream. He mentions that he…"tingled with fire not only from my groin but the back of my neck, my heart and the pit of my stomach. My whole body thrilled like in dreams of flying." This more than anything else he mentions indicates, that this might be an occurrence of "astral projection." The tingling sensation in the groin, solar plexus, heart and medulla areas could be indicative of the activated chakkra phenomena which supposedly accompanies an out-of-body experience. He even mentions dreams of flying, allegedly the most commonly experienced form of astral projection.

Most likely, early on in the experience, the "dreamer", if male, is fully erect or, if female, has begun to discharge vaginally. Unencumbered by the physical body and the time/space problems that gravity, clothing or bedding sometimes present, self-consciousness and inhibitions are completely absent. The seducer often talks and behaves in an extremely provocative and lewd manner. This is consistent with ancient reports. This is at first erotically irresistible and adds to the excitement and stimulation. But usually, before the encounter is over, becomes frighteningly disgusting.

Third and most strikingly consistent in both modern and ancient accounts of Succubi, is the inevitable discovery that the "lover" is not a woman. "She" is either found to possess a penis (or several of them) or as in my patient's tale, possessed no vagina or opening at all. Many experts on Incubi/Succubi go so far as to insist that there are not two types (sexes) of spirits at all, but only one non-sexual or hermaphroditic entity. Once this discovery is made and the Succubus unmasked, all pretense at disguise is abandoned and there is a desperate attempt to consummate the union and force ejaculation. This sometimes coincides with actual emission of semen but often a variety of "phantom" ejaculation takes place which delights the Succubus but leaves the victim drained of energy and sometimes painfully frustrated. How many times have we awakened in the morning feeling more tired and drained of energy than when we went to bed?

CHAPTER ELEVEN

MAGICKAL CHILDREN

How many times have you heard a person say that they hope they will have a boy or a girl? Have you ever heard someone say that they hope their child will be intelligent, have blond hair, brown eyes?

Have you heard of women who use special douches, eat certain foods, make offerings to gods, in order to conceive or receive a special child?

Have you known people who name their children to either honor a dead relative or name their children in order that other people will respond to them in a special way?

Well, Sex Magicians use their art to both conceive as well as to "bring in" or create a certain force in the Universe. Some religious authorities believe that this is how evil is brought into the world. The minds of the parents are on some thought or feeling which evokes or invokes a force to take shape in the womb.

From the Sex Magician's point of view, relying on chance or meager hopes in matters as important as this is criminal. Instead, the Sex Magician takes an active part in creating the type of child which he or she desires.

The procedure for creating a "magickal child" can be very simple or very complicated depending on the knowledge and needs of the Sex Magician.

A common procedure is to simply use Astrology or Tarot for determining the right times to conceive. For example, if the couple wanted a child with the qualities of Mercury they would wait until Mercury was direct and well aspected.

More complex methods such as the one described in *Secrets of Western Tantra,* or *Enochian Sex Magick* (New

Falcon Press, 1989, 1991) can involve months or perhaps years of preparation depending on the force and accuracy desired. If a couple wanted to "bring in" a Christ force it might take years to create the energy necessary to accomplish this task.

The same might hold true for a darker force, such as Hitler. Yes, some Sex Magicians are at this very moment preparing themselves to bring in evil or dark forces. Some people have even said that Hitler was brought into the world through violent thoughts generated during intercourse and coupled with suggestibility. The reader will have to decide for himself on these issues, whether thoughts, rituals, hopes, desires and fears can have an effect on conception.

Again, the reader will be aware that the definition of evil is a function of intention as well as the type of force a person desires to create. The Sex Magician believes he can accomplish intentionally the same event that a non-Sex Magician can do by mistake, accident, or just by being "normal" and "allowing God" to decide what type and kind of child you shall have.

The issue of the evil of Sex Magick is the idea of man taking the place of God. Thus, the alert reader can see why religion has always been against Magic as well as Science. Both methods can be used by Man to force his Will on the World Order. Of course there are as many arguments attempting to integrate Science with Religion. In fact, this nervous marriage has taken place, but to my knowledge the marriage between our present religions and Sex Magick has not taken place. Why?

Sex Magick is intentional, similar to science, but, there is no community, no outward control over the Sex Magician's behavior. His sexual sacrifices are not for his family, his god, his neighbor, nor his culture, but for life itself. In this sense he requires no sanction from his "tribe." This for many, particularly the middle class is the "Ultimate taboo."

The Sex Magician is more aware than most that he is a creator of life. Thus, having children is not a simple biological act, nor is it a religious duty to some God.

Creating life is God. For the Sex Magician the act of making another human is the ***making of a Universe.*** Thus, the life he creates is more sacred, more holy, than a normal person creates. His new creation is of and for Life, not for the State or the family mythos. This puts the Sex Magician somewhat outside the "normal" realm of society.

Of the practicing Sex Magicians I have met I have not found one to be psychopathic, schizophrenic or manic-depressive. Nor have I found them to suffer from either low or borderline intelligence.

Whether in fact their sexual magick works by our standards, what I have observed is their persistence in perfecting their techniques. Many of them are continually on the lookout for more sophisticated ways of making their art more joyous and powerful.

Throughout the entire conception and gestation process the Sex Magician takes care to continue to perform his rituals, including the preparation special Elixirs. It is believed by many Sex Magicians that the vaginal fluids contain sacred elements which can be used for very special rituals. This idea might stimulate in the reader's mind the idea of the curative powers of the embryo. Even today some health and healing medicines are made from embryos and other birth parts. The fear of intentional abortion of the human fetus is partially tied up with the belief that the human embryo contains great power.

The Magical use of the Elixir created during pregnancy could range from what we consider good to what we would consider evil.

I once met a woman who came to see me about her husband collecting the juices of their love making during pregnancy. It seems that prior to her pregnancy he would have oral sex with his wife after ejaculation. She thought nothing of this, however, after he found out that she was pregnant he began to collect the "vibrant love juices" in a bottle. He would run off afterwards and hide the mixture. When she asked him what he did with it, he said that he was saving it for a special occasion. His behavior so disturbed his wife that she refused to have sex with him. When he came in to visit me I asked him how he learned about this ancient practice. He responded that the thought just popped into his head. He thought the mixture at this time of her pregnancy had special powers, particularly during certain phases of the moon. It is particularly important to remember that these people had no interest at all in occultism.

Other than this behavior, I found nothing unusual about this man. He was quite successful as well as educated. I convinced the wife that his behavior was harmless and to go along with the gag; after all it wasn't hurting anyone.

I had another case quite opposite of this one. In this case it was the wife who wanted her husband to have oral sex with her after he had orgasm. Prior to her pregnancy this never crossed her mind, but even before she found out she was pregnant she began insisting that he collect the fluid with his mouth and share it with her. He thought she was going mad, however, I assured him that there was nothing wrong with her. I told him to humor her if he could and that in a short while her desire would change. I was wrong. Throughout her pregnancy she insisted on doing this, as she believed that the force in the fluid would enhance the embryo as well as herself. After she had the baby this behavior dropped of its own accord. As in the above case this couple had no interest in Sex Magick. Both had college degrees, never used drugs and were successful in their careers.

The experienced Sex Magician would see these behaviors of average, normal people as amateurish attempts to practice Sex Magick. He would know how much work and concentration goes into creating the Elixir as well as invoking the correct forces to cause the desired effect.

CHAPTER TWELVE

ORGASM AND GENETIC ECOLOGY THE WAY OF TANTRA AND THE MAGICKAL CHILD

There is a mysterious and divine power in the Will of every human. If it is not called into life by means of discipline and Will it atrophies and in the end dies. This is the process of normal life, to create a little and die. For most of us this process is all one small life can tolerate and for that matter maybe the planet cannot tolerate more. However, for some there is a different calling, sometimes seen as madness, or a great love, or a devotion to Life—to die in creating beyond one's own limits. Maybe it is a gift from the gods or a curse—I cannot say.

What greater natural force is there in the Universe than the will to create? And what greater means is there than sex, the most ordinary and common means accessible to just about everyone. To quote a noted Master, "Sex is, directly or indirectly, the most powerful weapon in the universe..." And just think, everyone has it—to disguise the great by making it common. Oh—great God—what a trick!

When discipline and sex are combined you transcend the ordinary.

By using Will, symbolism and ritual you touch the greatest force of the Universe never sought by ordinary humans.

You at once awaken the highest powers in yourself and transform yourself into a conscious evolutionary agent. This is the Essence of the Great Work, to transform yourself from an ordinary human to a God or Goddess. In order for this to take place you need the fuel which is the "ordinary" sexual drive freed from repression, access to the Will, and the symbols of the transformational process. When these are combined together, in just the right way, the adventure into the Numinous begins.

When you begin to love with such devotion and intensity—when you can no longer hold on to anything—then, and only then does the Child appear.

The Magickal Child is the New Human born not out of simple biology but out of the "madness" of Love itself. However, to experience this Love you first must learn to let go. This is not a moral dictate as told to us by our religions but nothing less than a necessity for planetary survival. Letting go is the greatest gift to the planet.

Letting go of yourself is the greatest Selfish act. To be this Selfish is to find one's No/thing/ness.

The Orgastic reflex can teach us freedom and the Magical Child can teach us to willingly suffer life, but **now** in a totally different way. Now we suffer, but we **are not** the suffering. Now we see the ego, but we **are not** the ego. Love must be No-Thing. You must sit in it, be absorbed by it until there is no difference between you and it. You must reek of its Divinity.

The Tantric act is a giving and a receiving. *There is no taking*. When giving and receiving reach their highest level of intensity then No-One is left. There is simply Love, **a Womb Without Walls.**

KARMA AND THE MANIFESTATION OF SOULS

Occultism has familiarized us with psychological practices of different kinds, all tending towards the eventual open manifestation of the spiritual faculties of the inner man. Nor is this all. Occultism has also presented us with such concepts as Reincarnation, various grades or types of

> souls who incarnate on this globe of ours, and the idea of karma determining amongst innumerable other things in what family and in what environment the incoming soul shall live.
> If human beings are spiritual beings, and thereby not exclusively subject to purely mechanical laws of heredity, is there a spiritual technique of eugenics as there is a physical technique observed by cattle breeders? To my knowledge this question has not hitherto been raised...

This was written by Israel Regardie sometime in the mid to late 30's and published in a occult journal in 1939. (Note: this article is included in Section Two of this book.)

It was not until the late 1970's that a plan was formulated combining bio-energetic techniques, which Regardie developed from Wilhelm Reich, the esoteric teachings of Secret Orders and Tantric practices. We believed that this "mixture" of ancient and modern wisdom would lead to the creation of the Magickal Child and Enlightenment.

The idea of creating a homonculus or a Magickal Child is ancient. The alchemists experimented with the homonculus idea for centuries. Even as late as the 1970's reports were circulated that some students of the late Frater Albertus had created life using alchemical means. I am not qualified to comment on the accuracy or validity of these reports; however, the idea of using Sexual practices for the purpose of Enlightenment and incarnating "souls" or psychic energies has been a goal of most magical orders.

The idea of creating or generating a race to heal the planet and help man to evolve is a desire as old as history itself.

In fact, influencing the characteristics of the foetus by incantations, prayer and other means is common. Some parents today for example use various means from douches, vitamins, concentration and hypnosis to influence the sex and characteristics of their offspring.

To quote Regardie:

> The really significant question however is this—can we, quite apart from sex, improve the quality of the child? That is to say, can we beforehand arrange that, just as a cow will have certain qualities that render it invaluable to breeders, the child will possess certain mental traits, emotional characteristics and abilities that will make it an asset to the human race? Personally, I believe we can.

USHERING IN THE GOLDEN AGE

In other words, Dr. Regardie believed that it was the responsibility of intelligent parents to elevate the planet by producing superior offspring.

He also felt that genetic manipulation was insufficient to accomplish this task since it couldn't take into account the spiritual nature of the "soul."

He felt that the psycho-spiritual mood in which a child was conceived would have a powerful effect on his/her future development. This is a fact that any psychotherapist will attest to—the mood of the parents during conception and during gestation determines much of the childs future.

In the process of producing superior offspring the parents would by necessity elevate their own consciousness. They would experience Orgastic Bliss. This experience is the prerequisite for the creation of the Magickal Child.

A ROMANCE BEYOND THE ROMANTIC

The goal of "Orgastic Thunder" was made possible by techniques handed down over the centuries, as well as those developed in *Secrets Of Western Tantra*, 1989 and elsewhere.

Orgastic thunder is not normal orgasm. It is an ecstasy which points its finger at Samadhi. It is a prolonged moment where the ego has wandered far away from its home.

The requirements to accomplish this are simple enough. First, the removal of the effects of repressive sexuality utilizing devotional practices. Second, the practice of certain meditations and rituals prior to and during sexual intercourse. The results are Orgastic Thunder and the creation of a Magickal vessel. The nature of the Magickal vessel can either take physical form or can remain as "spiritual energy" which can be utilized for healing, obtaining knowledge from higher sources, or as a bio-spiritual vehicle for the containment of the "parents" soul during times of danger or death.

As this process continues pre-genital intercourse is practiced which speeds up the process of de-armoring. Once the fundamental "ripples" of Kundalini begin to move, the couple begins to practice Tantric Intercourse using various symbols as they move through the Chakkras.

When they have reached a certain stage of awareness they begin to circulate the energy and release it into the **Sahasrara** Chakkra during Orgasm.

THE EROTIC SPIRIT
WITH THREE THERE IS ONE

One goal of Sex Magick is the uniting of opposites. However, this ultimate act of Love must be under the guidance of Will.

During the Melt Down process of the ego the couple utilizes the assumption of various God-Forms. This hastens the transformation of ordinary sexual union into an Archetypal embrace.

When the couple has become adept at these practices they begin to select the characteristics they wish to instill into the Magickal Child. Once this is accomplished they begin their work to reach the final and highest stage of the effort, the creation of the Magickal Child and their own enlightenment.

This entire process is designed to elevate the couple to divinity. They become Rex and Regina, the God and Goddess, merged as one in Orgastic Samadhi.

The evolutionary qualities of this process have barely been touched upon. The couple as Archetypical Lovers become the guiding force of Karmic evolution. Through the "sacrifice" of the personal they bring about a change in the energy forces of the planet. No longer are they concerned with the blind feeding frenzy of ordinary life. They have transformed themselves into food for the Divine. This is truly *Bliss Consciousness*.

CHAPTER THIRTEEN

THE BLACK MASS

Few subjects in literature titillate the imagination more than the Black Mass. We are presented with a nightmare image of an evil, defrocked Priest chaunting obscene paeans to the Prince of Darkness while a voluptuous nude woman (probably drugged to semiconsciousness) lies with legs spread-eagled, serving as the altar. Above her, hanging upside down, is a large crucifix. The soles of each foot of the Priest is tattooed with a crucifix so each step he takes necessitates his treading upon the Holy symbol.

The congregation is also naked, or perhaps wearing hooded robes opened in front so as to expose the genitals. They sway in an hypnotic wave and flawlessly intone a sinister chant while the Priest blasphemously parodies every segment of the Roman Catholic Mass.

The darkened church is lit by black candles made from the fat of babies or the of enemies of the "Church." The Host (a blackened turnip, cut into a triangular shape) is "consecrated" by inserting it in the open vagina of the "naked altar." The sacramental "wine" is the urine of a prostitute or perhaps the blood of a sacrificed baby.

The ceremony climaxes in a chaotic frenzy with acts of flagellation, masturbation, fellatio and cunnilingus culminating with the Priest sexually violating the "naked altar" with every unnatural act of perversion imaginable. Next the congregation does the same to her and to each other. In the midst of this madness the Devil himself appears and presents his grotesque backside to receive the obscene "kiss" of the devotees.

At the risk of disabusing many people who wish to believe such things are or were commonplace, we must say that there is very little evidence that such activities exist outside the minds of the writers of fiction or credulous religious zealots.

This is not to say that monstrous crimes have not been committed in the name of the Devil. The 17th Century excesses of Jeanne-Marie Bouvier (Madame Guyon) and Catherine Deshayes (La Voisin) are archetypical examples of the "messe noir" genre, but they by no stretch of the imagination constitute an orthodoxy of organized Devil worship.

The antics of Sir Francis Dashwood's "harmless but naughty" Hell-Fire Club of the mid 18th Century were not at all in the same league as the above French ladies. On the contrary, there is no evidence to indicate any crime was committed or anyone was ever harmed by his witty combination of sex, blasphemy and just plain fun.

The Black Mass whether real or imagined cannot be easily defined as a form of Sex Magick. In fact these images and rituals could be more accurately defined as a form of Christianity itself, the elements of which are simply reversed. The "Devil," not being a spiritual entity in himself outside of the doctrines of the Church, literally has become an averse "God" of the Christian Pantheon.

CHAPTER FOURTEEN

MAGICK MENSES

And if any man's semen pass from him, then he shall bathe all his flesh in water, and be unclean until the evening. And every garment, and every skin on which the semen shall be, shall be washed with water and be unclean until the evening. And a woman with whom a man lies with an emission of semen shall bathe with water, and be unclean until the evening. And if a woman's discharge in her flesh is a flow of blood, she shall be in her impurity seven days; and whoever touch her shall be unclean until the evening. And anything that she lies on in her impurity shall be unclean; and anything that she sits on shall be unclean. And whoever touch her bed shall wash his clothes and bathe in water, and be unclean until the evening...And if it is on the bed, or anything on which she sits when he touches it he shall be unclean until the evening. And if any man lies with her, and her impurity is on him, he shall be unclean seven days, and every bed on which he lies shall be unclean.

Jehovah, Leviticus XV

There exists a composite agent, at once natural and divine, corporal and spiritual, a universal plastic mediator, a common receptacle for the vibrations of movement and the images of form, a fluid and a force which may be termed in a certain sense the imagination of nature.

E. Levi (*op. cit.*)

The Blood is the life, Mr. Renfield.

Dracula

Besides combining divine images and sexual acts, another important part of Sex Magick is the use of sexual fluids as "holy water" and as objects of communion.

Yogis teach that blood is the vehicle of Prana, the life force of the universe which enters the body primarily through the breath and secondarily by way of food and water. Fresh blood containing this living "breath of life" or the Holy Spirit, is considered taboo even now among Orthodox Jews and some Muslims. A Kosher animal must be drained of its blood before it is cooked and eaten. In earlier times this blood was returned to the earth by pouring it into the soil or a stream. This practice of giving back the soul or life of the animal was said to keep the womb of the earth fertile.

In the ancient Roman Lupercalia festival held every February 15th, the blood and strips of skins of sacrificed goats were born by runners around the Palatine. Women would place themselves along the course to be hit by the bloody thongs to assure their fertility.

Menstrual blood was considered a powerful magical substance. "Wild indeed," says Pliny (1 A.D.), "are the stories told of the mysterious and awful power of the menstrual discharge." Menstrual blood was credited with a fearful power, an uncleanliness to be avoided, as well as many wonderful healing powers—the blood which flowed from the womb was both creative and destructive.

Menses was distinguished from other blood by its darker color. It appeared to lack the oxygenation of other blood. The dark color of menses became associated with powers of fertility, and so the colors of crimson, purple and violet became royal colors. As the Arthurian myths tell us, "The King and the Land are One." A wounded, impotent King is reflected by an infertile "Wasteland." Kings wore purple to insure the fertility of their land. The destructive power of menses was put to positive use by certain peoples. Menstruating women would be asked to walk or dance through the cornfields with their skirts raised or naked in order to kill such pests as caterpillars, worms and beetles. In other cultures the fear of menstruating women is so intense that they are quarantined and untouchable.

Today the fertile magic power of menstrual blood is being recognized once again. Some members of Goddess cults use the magick menses for love Philtres and even to fertilize their gardens.

CHAPTER FIFTEEN

SPERM AS A DRUG

> The Great Agent of the sun's operation is that force described in the symbol of Hermes on the Emerald Table; it is universal magic power, it is the igneous spiritual motor, the Jewish Od, and the Astral Light according to the expression adopted in this work. It is the secret, living, philosophical fire of which no Hermetic philosopher speaks, save with the most mysterious reserves; it is the universal sperm, the secret of which they guarded, merely representing it under the figure of the caduceus of Hermes.
>
> E. Levi (*op. cit.*)

The first time I heard of a breast enhancement "drug" or the Mexican "growth drug" was from a sailor in San Diego. He told me that he had learned about it when he went to Mexico and visited a whorehouse. One of the women told him that she liked to swallow the "manly juices" because it made her breasts grow. I was only seventeen at the time so I believed just about anything I was told about sex. I decided to go with him next time he went to the whorehouse and find out for myself.

Two months later I was in a border town in a Mexican bar talking to three or four "girls." As each was claiming special knowledge in various techniques, the joyful competition grew louder and louder until one of the girl's lack of tolerance for alcohol began to show. She started forcing herself on my friend saying over and over again in broken English something about the "juice" and how it made her feel strong. I listened for a few moments hoping to find out more. Finally, I decided that either her ideas were "crazy" or her discussion of manly juices was simply a device to turn the sailor on. As the couple left the bar I was escorted by a young lady to a room where the sailor and his girl had gone. The room was somewhat dark and I could see numerous shadowy couples moving and I heard groaning in broken English. What interested me most was the number of different women talking about the "juices" and the strength that it gave them. I decided that they were all crazy until their ideas stimulated certain memories of conversations between boys in my high school class. Some had spoken about this idea which they had learned from prostitutes in the local area. One even went so far as to say that a prostitute told him that a customer used to like to ejaculate and then engage in oral sex with her. She told my high school friend that this guy had to be a homosexual.

Many years later a psychologist friend of mine told me of his experiences in Mexico. An anthropologist and he went to Mexico to test prostitutes with the Herman Rorschach test. After testing, the prostitutes told them stories of the power of semen and in particular how it made their breasts grow.

The next time I heard about the "special" use of sperm was when an artist friend of mine got drunk during college and told me how he ejaculated into a bottle and mixed the sperm with his paints. Then he told me of how he would use this special paint to give a particular "holiness" or feeling to what he was painting. He said, "the painting comes alive when I use this magic paint." While I was shocked by this, my interest was again peaked and memories began to return again from my adolescence of how my peers used to talk about their sperm.

While these experiences can be explained away as adolescent experiences and the babble of "primitives," the next experience can not be easily explained away by such platitudes.

CHAPTER SIXTEEN

THE ELIXIR OF LIFE

ΚΕΦΑΛΗ ΙΗ

DEWDROPS

Verily, love is death, and death is life to come.
Man returneth not again; the stream floweth not uphill; the old life is no more; there is a new life that is not his.
Yet that life is of his very essence; it is more He than all that he calls He.
In the silence of a dewdrop is every tendency of his soul, and of his mind, and of his body; it is the Quintessence and the Elixir of his being. Therein are the forces that made him and his father and his father's father before him.
This is the Dew of Immortality.
Let this go free, even as It will; thou art not its master, but the vehicle of It.

Frater Perdurabo
The Book Of Lies (Samuel Weiser 1989)

One day I was introduced to a graduate engineer who took an almost immediate liking to me. After a few months of casual friendship, knowing that I was an expert in sexual pathology, he asked me if I knew what the Elixir of Life was. I told him that I had heard certain rumors. He asked me to tell him what I knew. I told him that this information was usually reserved for initiates of certain magickal and mystical societies. He giggled, saying that most of their secrets were nothing more than common knowledge taboos. I waited for a few moments when he told me of a strange practice he performed during certain times of the year. He would perform some strange and elaborate ritual and ejaculate into a glass. Afterwards he pricked his finger and drew some blood. He gently mixed these in a pan under slow heat adding a bit of special salt and pure grain alcohol. He would cook the brew for an hour or more. When it cooled he put the mixture into a bottle and placed it in the refrigerator. After a day or two he would drink small amounts of this Elixir when he felt weak or simply wanted to invigorate himself.

While the reader might feel strained or repulsed by such behavior, from a seemingly normal and successful engineer, a physicist told me a similar story. In his case he was attempting to create a homonuclus (a living creature which he fed with his own blood and sperm).

In investigating the mixing of blood and sperm to create an Elixir one is reminded of the Body and Blood of God. This ritual is performed continually in the open by today's Catholic and Orthodox Churches. Can we imagine that these otherwise normal individuals learned to perform their rituals by observing the Church's ritual or does the idea of the Elixir of Life and its relationship to body fluids go deeper than this superficial analysis?

Many magical and mystical societies have at their base strange and unusual sexual practices which include creating a mixture similar to the one our engineer created. They regard this mixture as a sacrament and use it under certain circumstances to perform other more developed magical rituals. Individuals who are aware of these secret methods, words and mixtures are usually the highest members of these Orders. Even in organizations which seem relatively normal, the members of the inner circle frequently have secret rituals which concern the use of blood, menses, sperm or other bodily fluids. Couples may copulate for hours and take the mixture of semen and vaginal secretions, mix them together with other ingredients and then consume the Elixir. In their "exalted" state they believe that they are achieving some form of spiritual transmutation of matter. No doubt the reader familiar with some of the symbols and methods of alchemy will feel at home with the symbolic aspects of these methods.

This is even true of some groups which insist that their symbols are purely symbolic. My investigation has revealed that symbols are frequently disguises for a deeper but more obvious reality.

In his book, *The Arcane Schools* (1909), John Yarker gives us a glimpse of some of the incredible Alchemical activities of an Eighteenth Century European Masonic lodge:

> The Count Joh. Ferd. Von Keuffstein, In Tyrol 1775, carried these bodies in bottles to the Lodge of which he was Master, where they were seen by Count Max. Lemburg, Count Franze Josef Von Thurn and others. These Homunculi were created by Keuffstein, and the Abbé Geloni, or Schiloni. Owing to the bottle being overturned one of the objects died, and the Count attempted to make another, but in the absence of the Abbé he only succeeded in making something of the nature of a leech, which soon died.

CHAPTER SEVENTEEN

THE EUCHARIST AND THE ELIXIR OF LIFE

The reader will immediately recognize the numerous taboos which these rituals violate, particularly ones concerning cannibalism. Is not the drinking of these liquids a symbolic act of eating the flesh and blood of another human or for that matter of God? In fact some Sex Magicians have orgasms with a particular God image in mind—screaming the name of these Gods at the top of their lungs during orgasm. Then they combine the fluids into a mixture, a sacrifice to this God, and drink the contents in a frenzied state of exaltation and excitement.

When I have relayed some of this information to otherwise normal people, I sometimes find them blushing, some later confessing that they too participated in similar behavior, never giving a thought to it except when they heard about someone else doing a similar thing. When I ask them how they learned these rituals, they often say that they do not see them as rituals but as natural and spontaneous acts.

In my experience every time I have heard about the Elixir it has been in a context of a religious sacrament or psychosexual pathology. This has motivated me to investigate further the Elixir of Life itself.

The Elixir, for short, is as old as human history. Groups have always believed that some magical mixture could be made from secret material to alleviate illness, bring enlightenment or render someone immortal or invisible. Many individuals, particularly those who are well educated, realize the symbolic quality of these myths. No one in their right mind can believe that by taking a mixture one can become invisible, cure disease, achieve enlightenment, or become immortal. This is utter nonsense to the modern educated mind. But is it? Think for a moment about certain modern drugs (Elixirs) which do some of the things mentioned. Now the reader will respond that my comparison is unfair and they are right. But, the idea of the Elixir is ancient and it is the belief of many Sex Magicians that we de-evolved from a higher and more powerful species with whom a few high initiates are in contact. Some believe that by making and ritually consuming sacred cakes composed of body fluids they are practicing an ancient and holy art.

It is believed that the essence of these higher races is contained in the blood, sperm and vaginal secretions. Some groups are so intent on this idea that they mix these together with other ingredients to form cakes and cookies which are used for medicinal and spiritual purposes. In fact some believe that life can be extended through a proper blend of these materials.

Normal psychosexual development presupposes a natural human process of the energization of body areas in a transformational and developmental fashion. In simple terms when you are an adult, the majority of your sexual pleasure must come from genital to genital contact. Not only is this developmentally sound, it is sound by all standards of modern religion. Like the Bible which forbids ejaculation except into the vaginal cavity, much of our modern standards hold that if an individual gain satisfaction more from oral, anal and or other activities his behavior would be regarded as abnormal or regressive. It is unfortunate that much of our scientific theorizing has been influenced by unsound insect biology and biblical inaccuracies.

Although the APA has removed homosexuality as a pathology from its list of deviations, it still has a quite extensive list of sexual pathology. Some of these are: Fetishism, Transvestism Zoophilia, Pedophilia, Exhibitionism, Voyeurism, Sexual Masochism and Sexual Sadism.

However, I can find no direct reference to Occult or Magickal Sexual Practices which include ritualized sexual behavior. This includes no references to the making or the drinking of the Elixir of Life, making love to God forms either in pairs or singularly. In fact there appears to be no pathological reference to these activities, except per chance as sub-behaviors of other pathologies such as Schizophrenia, Manic-Depressive Psychosis or Paranoia. It is also possible that these behaviors are observed in mental retards or in brain injured patients.

The question is how can otherwise normal individuals participate in such behavior?

CHAPTER EIGHTEEN

THE TALISMAN: MAKING THE DEAD LIVE

The making of talismans is an ancient art which relies upon the primitive belief that energy can be invested in an otherwise inanimate object. Even in modern times some people prefer things which are hand made because of the "love" and human effort that went into making it. Most people, however, are satisfied with manufactured items and store-bought gifts.

Talismans are devices which the magician makes to accomplish specific tasks such as creating fortune, harming an enemy, protecting against harm, attracting a lover etc. The magician uses colors, shapes and other materials harmonious or sacred to the force he wishes to evoke, to construct the talisman which he "charges" with a specific energy. He then either carries the talisman or puts it in a secret place. Some of the most powerful talismans are charged with the sexual energy created by passionate love making. Some magicians not only charge the talismans in this fashion but use the "Elixir" to make the talisman's effect even stronger.

CHARGING OF A TALISMAN WITH ELIXIR
A CONTEST OF WILL AND BODY

Several years ago I was introduced to a high ranking Freemason who surprised me with his interest in my work. He took delight in informing me that there existed a group of Middle Eastern origin, who were practicing religious sex, as he called it. He said they regularly performed an operation which appears to be a perfect example of the use of the Elixir to charge a Talisman or Link.

Often days of preparation are involved. The individuals are usually in excellent health and have developed their powers of concentration to a degree which enables them to perfectly hold in their minds the image of the object of the operation. The proponents of this ritual believe that it lends itself to a form of self-renewal although my friend said he had not seen any evidence of this in the people who claim to practice this ritual.

The couple, usually male and female, concentrate intensely on the object of the operation prior to starting the actual physical act.

The couple then enflame themselves in prayer as they focus upon the object and purpose of the operation. Often, mantras appropriate to the nature of the operation are used to focus the mind.

During the entire physical part of the ritual, which I have been told lasts as much as five hours, (although one hour is often enough) the mind and will must be directed towards the purpose of the operation.

It is obvious that the conflict between the desire to concentrate on the operation and the desire to consummate orgasm is immense. When orgasm is reached, the mind and the Will drop, and the fluids of the couple fuse. This is what they call the Elixir—sometimes thought of as the Medicine of Metals or the Quintessence.

It is believed the closer the male and female experience orgasm the better the operation.

The male collects the Elixir orally and shares it as a kiss with the female. The Elixir is not swallowed but absorbed through the membranes of the mouth in the same manner in which the Communion Wafer is allowed to melt in the mouth of the Western Christian communicant. Some of the "holy Elixir" is saved or reserved for the Talisman or the Magickal Link. This part of the Elixir is placed, smeared, etc. on the object in question. (See Chapter Twenty Eight for further details.)

When a talisman is made or a demon evoked for any purpose such as finding a lost object, acquiring wealth or to do harm or damage to another, the Sex Magician usually chooses a particular time when certain energy forces are active. When the time is right he protects and sanctifies the space where the charging is to take place. Once this is done, he alone, or with his lover begins to make passionate love, frequently screaming the names of Gods or demons until orgasm is reached. At that moment the intensity of the orgasm is focused on the talisman or the demon. After a few moments of rest the magician takes the Elixir and places a drop of it on the talisman or on the "sigil" (the signature) of the demon he is evoking.

The effect of placing animate material on inanimate matter is to vivify the talisman with the creative force of the Universe.

When these operations are complete other magickal acts are performed during very specific times to send the forces deeper into the Universe to do their work.

While some people might have difficulty in believing that such things as I have just described go on in the modern world, the reader will simply have to ask himself how this differs in kind from people praying to God for help, or for objects, or for that matter praying for the safety of a warrior or one side of a conflict to win and the other side to lose.

One difference is, of course, the prayer is always thought in the end to be the will of God and not the will of the person praying.

Love for the Sex Magician is not a philosophy or moral system but simply a force like any other force. He considers the power generated by conscious passion is the most powerful force in the Universe.

The reason it is possible for the Magician to use Love to do harm is his knowledge that Love is a force which he, like a thermostat, can increase or decrease depending upon his desire or Will.

This is very important in deciding whether something is "moral" or not. If damage occurs to someone because of the will of God then the damage is moral. If, however, the damage is a result of a person's will, then the person is regarded as immoral or evil. Intention is the primary reason why magick, and Sex Magick in particular, is erroneously assumed to be connected with Devil worship. It is the "willfulness" of the magician which is regarded as evil. If it is the will of God then there is no evil no matter how much damage is done by human standards.

CHAPTER NINETEEN

THE SEX MAGICIAN

In order not to mislead the reader I must emphasize that I have discovered that creating the Elixir and using it in magickal rituals is not the only goal of Sex Magicians. Nor is it understood or utilized by many who consider themselves Sex Magicians.

Some Magicians use Sex to create a force or energy which they believe normal sexual activity can not create. Others use Sex Magick to develop self-control, discipline and will power.

In fact some Sex Magicians, whether male or female, feel that they are more human, more moral than "normal" people, who blindly have intercourse, having no idea of what they are doing. They feel that normal people do not take the care they do in creating children. They feel that normal people misuse the most powerful source in the Universe—*the transmission of DNA from one human to another to create life.*

The Sex Magician frequently regards "normal" people as the Frankenstein monster: unconscious and full of repression, guilt, rage, ignorance and the arrogance brought on by consensus. It is interesting that these are the same attitudes normal people have about Sex Magick. I must leave it to the reader to decide who is more intolerant and ignorant.

There is no doubt that there is no direct scientific evidence that Sex Magick does anything that it claims. In fact there are probably no scientific studies to compare Sex Magicians with non-Sex Magicians. It does seem, however, that the Sex Magician attempts to integrate passion with consciousness, while normals seem to ritualize their sex behavior a bit differently. Frequently, "normals" have times and places where they have sex. This is particularly true as a couple becomes more familiar with each other. Sex under these circumstances frequently takes on mechanical and obsessive characteristics, possessing neither consciousness nor passion.

In 1987, I had the opportunity to meet a Sex Magician of rather high repute who agreed to answer a few questions. We went to a nice restaurant, had a few cups of coffee, switched to espresso, then red wine. I asked him what he thought Sex Magick was. He responded that Sex Magick was the oldest religion on the planet. By religion he told me he meant 'awe of life.' Sex Magick was the union of Will and Passion. It was the Cup from which the Wise drank. Every idea about immaculate conception is based on the principles of Sex Magick—bringing "a god force" into the womb. This is an old story of which Jesus was simply a bad example—which attracted slaves, the power mad and the weak. All god-men, he said, were made by Sex Magick whether intentionality or accidently. In some cases, he dilated, *outside forces come into a womb simply because no-one performed the correct ritual to keep them out.* I tried to interrupt him but he pushed my sounds aside. He said that much of what the world calls evil is the result of not practicing Sex Magick consciously. *That is, strong spirits are forcing themselves into manifestation. If Sex Magick were employed by those people who are concerned with their ideas of "Good and Evil" there would be less evil in the world.* He claimed that Hitler was the result of a highly suggestive womb and a violent father. He added, that he was well aware that other forces were operating, which included the mass repression of 'darkness' which the world at large was undergoing.

CHAPTER TWENTY

OF EATING BLOOD AND IDOL WORSHIP

The Mosaic Law implies that statues, paintings and idols elicit an "evil inclination." Part of the "evil inclination" is the erotic response. The other is the danger that the sexual response could somehow vivify the image by linking it to blood sacrifice.

The fear that a fixed image could be projected upon the fertile, living medium of blood and that it could in fact create a new lifeform, is the foundation of both the Mosaic blood taboos and the proscription of graven images.

What God did not want man to do was to create in the imagination—for that was the first step to creating in actuality—a trick reserved for God alone.

Recently on a Christian talk-radio program an "expert" on early childhood education cautioned Christian parents on the dangers of "the Imagination." His contention was that children possessed a powerful imagination, not as a gift from God but as unholy temptation from Satan. Role-playing games and pretending were especially to be forbidden as they lure children deeper and deeper into the false world of the imagination (identified by this "expert" as Hell), where they can discover that "thoughts themselves are creative." This "expert" went so far as to maintain that this ability was the underlying cause of the Fall of Man.

Misguided as the above "expert" was, he did perceive the underlying truth of Sex Magick, that the powers of the imagination are indeed dangerously close to the Divine creative force. From the Sex Magician's point of view, to purposely attempt to suppress this wonderful, natural ability in one's own children is a despicable form of child abuse.

Blood sacrifice among the Hebrews, and later among the Christians, evolved over the centuries in a most interesting progression: Abraham was a Godly man. Obedience to God in his day required human sacrifice, specifically the sacrifice of the first born male child. This he was prepared to do when it was "revealed" to him that a first-born male *animal* could be substituted for the human child.

The Eucharist of the Last Supper further substituted the flesh and blood of the animal sacrifice with bread and wine.

We start with Human Blood—the perfect Child.

Next, Human parts—Circumcision—The Blood of the Penis.[1]

Next, Animal Blood—the perfect animal.

Next, Food—Bread/Wine—Earth and Sun—no longer blood.

Missing here is Sperm and Vaginal fluids which are a more advanced form of the primitive blood.

The Elixir is used as a symbol of Light and Life. The Earth is the Egg and the Sun the Sperm.

As such, Sex Magick is a rung on a Universal Ladder of creation. It is the fruit of the Knowledge of Good and Evil. Procreation, and creation have been reserved by God himself. If you are not allowed to use blood or hold an image in your mind you are cut off from the Art of transmutation. It is taken from the hands of man and placed in the hands of the priest. From the Sex Magician's point of view the priest appears to be acting as a broker for a

---

[1] There is a story still circulating today that during the 11th and 12th centuries A.D. that upon circumcision the child's penis was sucked by the person performing the circumcision to insure that all the blood was drained. It is also rumored that some groups waited until the boy was thirteen years old before this operation was performed.

voracious demon and not the representative of a Universal Deity.

Contrast this idea to the Mithraic initiation ceremonies where the candidate was washed in the blood of the sacrificial bull or its surrogate and encouraged to consume it eucharistically. The animal was slain upon a grating which covered a pit where the naked candidate was placed.

> Through the open grating the bloody dew flows into the pit; the neophyte receives the falling drops on his head and body, he leans back so that his cheeks, lips and nostrils are wetted; he pours the liquid over his eyes and does not even spare his mouth, for he moistens his tongue with blood and sips it eagerly.
> *Prudentius (A.D. 390)*

SECTION II

Modern Sex Magicians
Secret Sex Rituals

CHAPTER TWENTY ONE

THE KNIGHTS TEMPLAR AND THE SEX MAGICIANS

The Order of the Knights Templar was founded in 1118 AD to defend the city of Jerusalem and to protect pilgrims on the way to the Holy Land. It was a religious and military Order and the Knights took vows of poverty, chastity, and obedience. They had a secret form of reception into their Order and were originally headquartered on the site of King Solomon's Temple, hence the name of Knights Of The Temple or Templars.

In spite of the Knight's individual vows of poverty, the Order as an institution eventually amassed great wealth while guarding the trade routes to the Middle East.

In 1307 the French Monarch Phillip le Bel initiated a brutal campaign of persecution against the Templars, seizing their persons and property and putting them on trial. The bizarre charges against them included sodomy, spitting or trampling upon the Cross and worshipping a skull or head called Baphomet.

Whatever the validity or invalidity of the charges against them, the Order was ruthlessly crushed in France and disbanded by Papal order in 1312. Some historians in the last few years have made a strong case for the survival of the Knights Templar and the Order's metamorphosis into Free Masonry. Whether or not this is the case, the name and legends of the Knights Templar inspired numerous Masonic degrees and rites from the mid-18th century on.

One of the most interesting groups founded on the romanticized Templar legends was conceived around 1895 by Dr. Karl Kellner, a wealthy Austrian paper chemist and industrialist. Kellner travelled extensively in Europe, America, and Asia Minor. It was during these travels that he was said (by his friend Theodore Reuss) to have come into contact with an organization called the Hermetic Brotherhood of Light.

As a result of this contact, Kellner was inspired to found an "Academia Masonica" (Masonic Academy) to preserve and teach "certain secrets" which he believed to be the key to the symbolism of Freemasonry, religion and nature. To assist him in this endeavor, Kellner chose his friend Theodore Reuss.

Reuss was a colorful man. He was born in Augsburg in 1855, the son of an innkeeper. A few months after his twenty-first birthday he became a Freemason, being initiated in Pilgrim Lodge Number 228 in London which worked in the German language. On January 9, 1878, he was raised to the 3rd degree of Master Mason. Reuss became a professional singer and journalist and was active for a time in Socialist politics until his leftist friends suspected him of being a Prussian spy.

Kellner and Reuss decided to call their order "Orientalische Templer" (The Order of the Templars of the East, or Ordo Templi Orientis or the O.T.O.). In 1902 they took steps to acquire a charter conferring powers to establish a body of the Ancient and Primitive Rite of Memphis and Mizraim. This organization, or permutations of it, had long been a thorn in the side of conventional Freemasonry. With its impressive number of degrees (33°, 90°, 95°) and an astounding array of titles including: Doctor Of The Planispheres, Sublime Sage Of The Zodiac, Pontiff Of Kneph, etc., etc., etc. it had a strong appeal to the curious, the serious Masonic researcher and the dilettante. Reuss and Kellner felt that it would provide a suitable structure for their purposes. The esoteric teachings of the Hermetic Brotherhood Of Light were reserved for an Inner Circle running parallel to the highest degrees of their Memphis and Mizraim Rite.

But just what was the nature of the "key" that Kellner discovered? Reuss made this very clear in his September, 1912 issue of the Oriflamme:

> Our Order possesses the **Key** which opens up all Masonic and Hermetic Secrets, namely the Teaching of Sexual Magic, and this Teaching explains, without exception, all the Secrets of Nature, all the symbolism of Freemasonry and all systems of Religion.

When Karl Kellner died at Vienna in 1905, Theodore Reuss became the head of the O.T.O. with all its Masonic aberrations, glorious titles and secret keys.

During his term of office as head of the O.T.O., Reuss issued many certificates and charters. Some of these would latter become an embarrassment to their bearers or their followers. The efforts to legitimize their own Orders in a labyrinth of charters and titles sometimes bit them smartly on their own taboos as the central theme of the O.T.O.'s "secret" became clear (and, some would say, immediately misunderstood).

Such was not the case with Aleister Crowley. Perhaps the most fateful step made by Reuss was his appointment in 1912 of Aleister Crowley as the head of the Order for Great Britain and Ireland. Crowley enthusiastically embraced the Order and brought to it all of his unique talents and knowledge.

When Reuss suffered a stroke in 1922, he named Crowley as his chosen successor to the Order. He died at Munich in October, 1923.

From Crowley's entrance into the O.T.O. in 1912 until his death in England in 1947, the Order played an important role in his life and work. The O.T.O. inspired him and he infused it with his Thelemic philosophy of Life, Love, Light and Liberty.

Today, the only legitimate successors of the original O.T.O. are headquartered in New York City. It is an

International Order with official bodies in Europe and Asia as well as the Americas.

In addition to working the traditional degrees of the O.T.O., many of the local bodies give classes in Yoga, Meditation, Qabalah and Ceremonial Magick. Several produce local bulletins and magazines. Many regularly perform Crowley's Gnostic Mass (See *Gems From The Equinox*, New Falcon, 1991). Also his series of plays, the Rites of Eleusis are regularly performed.

While carefully preserving Crowley's legacy, the Order is in the forefront of promoting the philosophy and work this heir of the Knights Templar.

CHAPTER TWENTY TWO

ALEISTER CROWLEY
THE WICKEDEST MAN IN THE WORLD?

> There is great danger in me; for who doth not understand these runes shall make a great miss. He shall fall down into the pit called Because, and there he shall perish with the dogs of Reason.
> Liber AL II, 27

He called himself the Beast 666. He appears to have boasted in print that he ritually "sacrificed" hundreds of children; a man who was accused of every form of atrocity imaginable, from the sinking of the Lusitania to choreographing the events that plunged the nations of the earth into the First World War. One account even makes him responsible for the death of Emilia Eharhart. He was a ruthless adventurer and mountaineer reported to have killed and *eaten* two of his native guides; a man who claimed to have destroyed the God of Christianity and announced a new religion some say was based on selfishness and spiritual anarchy.

His name was Aleister Crowley and the newspaper headlines of the day called him:

"The King Of The Devil Cults, The Purple Priest, A Human Beast, A Cannibal At Large, A Man We'd Like to Hang, The Wickedest Man In The World".

Mussolini ordered him expelled from Sicily. He was also expelled from France. British Customs seized and destroyed books he had authored and chaos, suicide and scandal followed in his wake.

The British weekly, the *Sunday Referee* (March 10, 1935) asked the question that over half a century later is only beginning to be answered.

> Who—and what—is Aleister Crowley? Around few men in contemporary life has been created such a wealth of fantastic fable and rumour as that which attaches to the name of this mysterious personality.

Who indeed was this man, and why, if it were true he was guilty of so many unspeakable acts, was he never brought to justice or ever formally charged with any crime?

To the modern student of Crowley, the answer to the second part of the question is simple. He was never charged with any crimes because there were no crimes to be charged with. And even if there were, to some, the magnitude and the importance of his work is such as to dwarf to insignificance an entire litany of personal flaws and excesses real or imagined.

In the opinion of some of our contemporaries, Crowley was a genius of stellar magnitude. Currently his works enjoy a scrutiny and popularity that never was achieved in his lifetime and are often seriously compared to those of Machiavelli, William Blake and Friedrich Nietzsche. He is hailed by some modern occultists as the greatest magician of the Twentieth Century.

His influence upon the modern occult and New Age movement is immeasurable and no matter what one's opinion of the man and his work may be, no study of modern religion or sexuality is complete without a basic understanding of Crowley.

In the early 1970's Israel Regardie, who served for several years as Crowley's secretary, wrote in *Eye in the Triangle* (Falcon Press, 1982)

His name has come to be associated with a blackguard, and adventurer, a mystic crackpot, and god knows what else. Yet in my sober estimation he may eventually turn out to be the greatest rebel of the lot. What he did and stood for may yet result in the complete about-face of all our values and general behavior. The events of our time are already pointing in this direction—and he has been dead for not more than a quarter of a century. His influence is far more subtle and indirect and yet all-pervasive than Blavatsky. James Branch Cabel's Jurgen used a number of Crowley's ideas and rituals without acknowledgement, and I fancy the current hippie bible, Robert Heinlein's *A Stranger in a Strange Land*, owes a very great deal to Aleister Crowley, though this too is unacknowledged. But a lot of other people are using his ideas quite freely without feeling obligated to mention his name. Crowley would not have minded this, so intent was he on shaking the foundations and the roofing of the social structure of our age.

He challenged unequivocally the basic religious attitudes of our society, stressing the idea of personal experience of God through the pursuit of time-honored paths and techniques. He was also an advocate of the occasional use of the psychedelic drugs as giving one a foretaste of the kind of experience to be aimed at by the employment of the magical and yogic techniques. Beyond these considerations, however, what he stood for was the total rejection of all our current moral values.

Taboo: The Ecstasy Of Evil

It is obvious to all who wish to seriously study Crowley, that he was clearly a man ahead of his time. It was obvious to him as well and so, to assure that his works would survive long enough to be appreciated, he systematically set to work to create a sinister and infamous international reputation for himself. Crowley had an intuitive sense of the value of imprinting. By imbedding intense shocks in the information he presented he was assured that there would be a lasting impression, either for good or ill, upon the mind of the reader. He succeeded admirably. His bizarre sense of humor and his admittedly eccentric life-style added much grist for the rumor mill. In fact, there is usually a kernel of truth in almost every fantastic accusation leveled at him.

This is especially true of his magical writings. Often, when referring to esoteric sexual applications or techniques, he "blinds" the naive with what appears to be the details of acts of black magic or human sacrifice when it is obvious to the sophisticated reader that he is simply referring to magical aspects of sexual activity that were bound to be misunderstood by the general public anyway. His attitude being: if only a handful of individuals will ever understand what is being written, write it in such a way that it will never go out of print.

The modern reader must also bear in mind that the transcendent nature of spiritual subject matter often can only be represented by images terrible and strange. Language is not representative of reality. That Crowley was a master of metaphor is unarguable. But what is more significant is his ability to utilize words and images in the same manner as the Zen Master's Koan; expressing what appears technically to be a logical formula of language in such a way as to force the mind of the reader to deal with realities that transcend logic.

The Hindu Goddess Kali presents a terrifying figure. She eats the souls of her devotees and is adorned with a necklace of their skulls. She is the terrible Goddess of Death, destruction and catastrophe. Yet Kali is the beloved symbol of the Mother Deity for millions of pious Hindus. Her worshippers are sincere, productive citizens and include both the humble and influential. They see nothing unusual or evil in the symbols surrounding their religious practices and are seldom if ever persecuted or criticized for their beliefs.

The Western mind is not generally ready to achieve such subtle levels of spiritual comprehension without a great deal of preparation and effort. We are blinded by our language. The Western mind has the uncanny ability of confusing language with reality. Something is either good or evil. Crowley used language to overcome language. His writings are often filled with shocking statements and images of death, violence and evil which challenge the reader to see the Deity that transcends God-and-the-Devil, the Divine that transcends the Holy-and-the-Unholy, the Life that transcends Good-and-Evil.

CHAPTER TWENTY THREE

THE BLOODY SACRIFICE

The following originally appeared in 1929 as Chapter Eleven of *Magick In Theory and Practice*. (The most recent edition is by Magickal Childe 1991). Perhaps no other piece of writing has added more to Crowley's reputation as a Black Magician. Portions of this chapter are often quoted even today by individuals wishing to prove that Crowley advocated and participated in acts of human sacrifice. We need only refer to the footnotes to realize that this is not the case.

This is a classic example of the type of literary blind that Crowley loved to utilize when he wished to publish, in a public medium, sensitive or secret information that had heretofore been reserved for high initiates while, at the same time, shocking and outraging the public at large.

Today the sexual connotations are obvious to all but the most mentally or emotionally disadvantaged. For such unfortunates we advise they read the last sentence of this chapter first:

"You are likely to get into trouble over this chapter unless you truly comprehend its meaning."

OF THE BLOODY SACRIFICE: AND MATTERS COGNATE.

By
The Master Therion
Aleister Crowley

It is necessary for us to consider carefully the problems connected with the bloody sacrifice, for this question is indeed traditionally important in Magick. Nigh all ancient Magick revolves around this matter. In particular all the Osirian religions—the rites of the Dying God—refer to this. The slaying of Osiris and Adonis the mutilation of Attis; the cults of Mexico and Peru; the story of Hercules or Melcarth; the legends of Dionysus and of Mithra, are all connected with this one idea. In the Hebrew religion we find the same thing inculcated. The first ethical lesson in the Bible is that the only sacrifice pleasing to the Lord is the sacrifice of blood; Abel, who made this, finding favour with the Lord, while Cain, who offered cabbages, was rather naturally considered a cheap sport. The idea recurs again and again. We have the sacrifice of the Passover, following on the story of Abraham's being commanded to sacrifice his firstborn son, with the idea of the substitution of animal for human life. The annual ceremony of the two goats carries out this in perpetuity. And we see again the domination of this idea in the romance of Esther, where Haman and Mordecai are the two goats or gods; and ultimately in the presentation of the rite of Purim in Palestine, where Jesus and Barabbas happened to be the Goats in that particular year of which we hear so much, without agreement on the date.

This subject must be studied in the "Golden Bough", where it is most learnedly set forth by Dr. J. G. Frazer.

Enough has now been said to show that the bloody sacrifice has from time immemorial been the most considered part of Magick. The ethics of the thing appear to have concerned no one; nor, to tell the truth, need they do so. As St. Paul says, "Without shedding of blood there is no remission"; and who are we to argue with St. Paul? But, after all that, it is open to any one to have any opinion that he likes upon the subject, or any other subject, thank God! At the same time, it is most necessary to study the business, whatever we may be going to do about it; for our ethics themselves will naturally depend upon our theory of the universe. If we were quite certain, for example, that everybody went to heaven when he died, there could be no serious objection to murder or suicide, as it is generally conceded—by those who know neither—that earth is not such a pleasant place as heaven.

However, there is a mystery concealed in this theory of the bloody sacrifice which is of great importance to the student, and we therefore make no further apology. We should not have made even this apology for an apology, had it not been for the solicitude of a pious young friend of great austerity of character who insisted that the part of this chapter which now follows—the part which was originally written—might cause us to be misunderstood. This must not be.

The blood is the life. This simple statement is explained by the Hindus by saying that the blood is the principal vehicle or vital Prana[1] There is some ground for the belief that there is a definite substance[2], not isolated as yet, whose presence makes all the difference between live and

---

[1] Prana or "force" is often used as a generic term for all kinds of subtle energy. The prana of the body is only one of its "vayus". Vayu means air or spirit. The idea is that all bodily forces are manifestations of the finer forces of the more real body, this real body being a subtle and invisible thing.

[2] This substance need not be conceived as "material" in the crude sense of Victorian science; we now know that such phenomena as the rays and emanations of radioactive substances occupy an intermediate position. For instance, mass is not, as once supposed, necessarily impermeable to mass, and matter itself can be only interpreted in terms of motion. So, as to "prana", one might hypothesize a phenomenon in the ether analogous to isomerism. We already know of bodies chemically identical whose molecular structure makes one active, another inactive to certain reagents. Metals can be "tired" or even "killed" as to some of their properties, without discoverable chemical change. One can "kill" steel, and "raise it from the dead"; and flies drowned in icewater can be resuscitated. That it should be impossible to create high organic life is scientifically unthinkable, and the Master Therion believes it to be a matter of few years indeed before this is done in the laboratory. Already we restore the apparently drowned. Why not those dead from such causes as syncope? If we understood the ultimate physics and chemistry of the brief moment of death we could get hold of the force in some way, supply the missing element, reverse the electrical conditions or what not. Already we prevent certain kinds of death by supplying wants, as in the case of Thyroid.

dead matter. We pass by with deserved contempt the pseudo-scientific experiments of American charlatans who claim to have established that weight is lost at the moment of death, and the unsupported statements of alleged clairvoyants that they have seen the soul issuing like a vapour from the mouth of persons *in articulo mortis;* but his experiences as an explorer have convinced the Master Therion that meat loses a notable portion of its nutritive value within a very few minutes after the death of the animal, and that this loss proceeds with ever-diminishing rapidity as time goes on. It is further generally conceded that live food, such as oysters, is the most rapidly assimilable and most concentrated form of energy.[3] Laboratory experiments in food-values seem to be almost worthless, for reasons which we cannot here enter into; the general testimony of mankind appears a safer guide.

It would be unwise to condemn as irrational the practice of those savages who tear the heart and liver from an adversary, and devour them while yet warm. In any case **it was the theory of the ancient Magicians, that any living being is a storehouse of energy varying in quantity according to the size and health of the animal, and in quality according to its mental and moral character.** At the death of the animal this energy is liberated suddenly.

---

[3] One can become actually drunk on oysters, by chewing them completely. Rigor seems to be a symptom of the loss of what I may call the Alpha-energy and makes a sharp break in the curve. The Beta and other energies dissipate more slowly. Physiologists should make it their first duty to measure these phenomena; for their study is evidently a direct line of research into the nature of Life. The analogy between the living and complex molecules of the Uranium group of inorganic and the Protoplasm group of organic elements is extremely suggestive. The faculties of growth, action, self-recuperation, etc., must be ascribed to similar properties in both cases; and as we have detected, measured and partially explained radioactivity, it must be possible to contrive means of doing the same for Life.

Psychopathology Of Sex And Religion

The animal should therefore be killed[4] within the Circle, or the Triangle, as the case may be, so that its energy cannot escape. An animal should be selected whose nature accords with that of the ceremony—thus, by sacrificing a female lamb one would not obtain any appreciable quantity of the fierce energy useful to a Magician who was invoking Mars. In such a case a ram[5] would be more suitable. And this ram should be virgin—the whole potential of its original total energy should not have been diminished in any way[6]. For the highest spiritual working one must accordingly choose that victim which contains the greatest and purest force. A male child of perfect innocence and high intelligence[7] is the most satisfactory and suitable victim.

For evocations it would be more convenient to place the blood of the victim in the Triangle—the idea being that the

---

[4] It is a mistake to suppose that the victim is injured. On the contrary, this is the most blessed and merciful of all deaths, for the elemental spirit is directly built up into Godhead—the exact goal of its efforts through countless incarnations. On the other hand, the practice of torturing animals to death in order to obtain the elemental as a slave is indefensible, utterly black magic of the very worst kind, involving as it does a metaphysical basis of dualism. There is, however, no objection to dualism or black magic when they are properly understood. See the account of the Master Therion's Great Magical Retirement by Lake Pasquaney, where He "crucified a toad in the Basilisk abode".

[5] A wolf would be still better in the case of Mars. See 777 for the correspondences between various animals and the "32 Paths" of Nature.

[6] There is also the question of its magical freedom. Sexual intercourse creates a link between its exponents, and therefore a responsibility.

[7] It appears from the Magical Records of Frater Perdurabo that He made this particular sacrifice on an average about 150 times every year between 1912 e. v. and 1928 e. v. Contrast J. K. Huyman's "LaBas", where a perverted form of Magic of an analogous order is described.

"It is the sacrifice of oneself spiritually. And the intelligence and innocence of that male child are the perfect understanding of the Magician, his one aim, without lust of result. And male he must be, because what he sacrifices is not the material blood, but his creative power." This initiated interpretation of the texts was sent spontaneously by Soror I.W E., for the sake of the younger Brethren.

spirit might obtain from the blood this subtle but physical substance which was the quintessence of its life in such a manner as to enable it to take on a visible and tangible shape.[8]

Those magicians who object to the use of blood have endeavored to replace it with incense. For such a purpose the incense of Abramelin may be burnt in large quantities. Dittany of Crete is also a valuable medium. Both these incenses are very catholic in their nature, and suitable for almost any materialization.

But the bloody sacrifice, though more dangerous is more efficacious; and for nearly all purposes human sacrifice is the best. The truly great Magician will be able to use his own blood, or possibly that of a disciple, and that without sacrificing the physical life irrevocably[9]. An example of this sacrifice is given in Chapter 44 of Liber 333. This Mass may be recommended generally for daily practice.

One last word on this subject. **There is a Magical Operation of maximum importance: the Initiation of a New Aeon. When it becomes necessary to utter a Word, the whole Planet must be bathed in blood. Before man is ready to accept the Law of Thelema, the Great War must be fought. This Bloody Sacrifice is the critical point of the World Ceremony of the Proclamation of Horus, the**

---

[8] See Equinox (I, V. Supplement: Tenth Aethyr) for an Account of an Operation where this was done. Magical phenomena of the creative order are conceived and germinate in a peculiar thick velvet darkness, crimson, purple, or deep blue, approximating black: as if it were said, In the body of Our Lady of the Stars.

See 777 for the correspondences of the various forces of Nature with drugs, perfumes, etc.

[9] Such details, however, may safely be left to the good sense of the Student. Experience here as elsewhere is the best teacher. In the Sacrifice during Invocation, however, it may be said without fear of contradiction that the death of the victim should coincide with the supreme invocation

Crowned and Conquering Child, as Lord of the Aeon.[10]

This whole matter is prophesied in the Book of the Law itself; let the student take note, and enter the ranks of the Host of the Sun.

II

There is another sacrifice with regard to which the Adepts have always maintained the most profound secrecy. It is the supreme mystery of practical Magick. Its name is the Formula of the Rosy Cross. In this case the victim is always—in a certain sense—the Magician himself, and the sacrifice must coincide with the utterance of the most sublime and secret name of the God whom he wishes to invoke.

Properly performed, it never fails of its effect. But it is difficult for the beginner to do it satisfactorily, because it is a great effort for the mind to remain concentrated upon the purpose of the ceremony. The overcoming of this difficulty lends most powerful aid to the Magician.

It is unwise for him to attempt it until he has received regular initiation in the true[11] **Order of**

---

[10] Note: This paragraph was written in the summer of 1911 e.v., just three years before its fulfillment.

[11] It is here desirable to warn the render against the numerous false orders which have impudently assumed the name of Rosicrucian. The Masonic Societas Rosicruciana is honest and harmless; and makes no false pretences; if its members happen as a rule to be pompous busy-bodies, enlarging the borders of their phylacteries, and scrupulous about cleansing the outside of the cup and the platter; if the masks of the Officers in their Mysteries suggest the Owl, the Cat, the Parrot, and the Cuckoo, while the Robe of their Chief Magus is a Lion's Skin, that is their affair. But those orders run by persons *claiming* to represent the True Ancient Fraternity are common swindles. The representatives of the late S. L. Mathers (Count McGregor) are the phosphorescence of the rotten wood of a branch which was lopped off the tree at the end of the 19th century. Those of Papus (Dr. Encausse), Stanislas de Guaita and Peladan, merit respect as serious, but lack full knowledge and authority. The "Ordo Rosae Crucis" is a mass of ignorance and falsehood, but this may be a deliberate device for masking itself. The

the Rosy Cross, and he must have taken the vows with the fullest comprehension and experience of their meaning. It is also extremely desirable that he should have attained an absolute degree of moral emancipation[12] and that purity of spirit which results from a perfect understanding both of the differences and harmonies of the planes upon the Tree of Life.

For this reason FRATER PERDURABO has never dared to use this formula in a fully ceremonial manner, save once only, on an occasion of tremendous import, when, indeed, it was not He that made the offering, but ONE in Him. For he perceived a grave defect in his moral character which he has been able to overcome on the intellectual plane, but not hitherto upon higher planes. Before the conclusion of writing this book he will have done so[13].

The practical details of the Bloody Sacrifice may be studied in various ethnological manuals, but the general conclusions are summed up in Frazer's "Golden Bough", which is strongly recommended to the reader.

Actual ceremonial details likewise may be left to experiment. The method of killing is practically uniform. The animal should be stabbed to the heart, or its throat severed, in either case by the knife. All other methods of killing are less efficacious; even in the case of Crucifixion death is given by stabbing[14].

---

test of any Order is its attitude towards the Law of Thelema. The True Order presents the True Symbols, but avoids attaching the True Name thereto; it is only when the Postulant has taken irrevocable Oaths and been received formally, that he discovers what Fraternity he has joined. If he have taken false symbols for true and find himself magically pledged to a gang of rascals, so much the worse for him!

[12] This results from the full acceptance of the Law of THELEMA, persistently put into practice.

[13] P. S. With the happiest results. P.

[14] Yet one might devise methods of execution appropriate to the Weapons: Stabbing or clubbing for the Lance or Wand, Drowning or

One may remark that warm-blooded animals only are used as victims: with two principal exceptions. The first is the serpent, which is only used in a very special Ritual;[15] the second the magical beetles of Liber Legis. (See Part IV.)

One word of warning is perhaps necessary for the beginner. The victim must be in perfect health—or its energy may be as it were poisoned. It must also not be too large:[16] the amount of energy disengaged is almost unimaginably great, and out of all anticipated proportion to the strength of the animal. Consequently, the Magician may easily be overwhelmed and obsessed by the force which he has let loose; it will then probably manifest itself in its lowest and most objectionable form. **The most intense spirituality of purpose**[17] **is absolutely essential to safety.**

In evocations the danger is not so great, as the Circle forms a protection; but the circle in such a case must be protected, not only by the names of God and the Invocations used at the same time, but by a long habit of successful

---

poisoning for the Cup, Beheading for the Sword, Crushing for the Disk, Burning for the Lamp, and so forth.

[15] The Serpent is not really killed; it is seethed in an appropriate vessel; and it issues in due season refreshed and modified, but still essentially itself. The idea is the transmission of life and wisdom from a vehicle which has fulfilled its formula to one capable of further extension. The development of a wild fruit by repeated plantings in suitable soil is an analogous operation.

[16] The sacrifice (e.g.) of a bull is sufficient for a large number of people; hence it is commonly made in public ceremonies, and in some initiations, e.g. that of a King, who needs force for his whole kingdom. Or again, in the Consecration of a Temple.

See Lord Dunsany, "The Blessing of Pan" — a noble and most notable prophecy of Life's fair future.

[17] This is a matter of concentration, with no ethical implication. The danger is that one may get something which one does not want. This is "bad" by definition. Nothing is in itself good or evil. The shields of the Sabines which crushed Tarpeia were not murderous to them, but the contrary. Her criticism of them was simply that they were what she did not want in her Operation.

Taboo: The Ecstasy Of Evil

defence.[18] If you are easily disturbed or alarmed, or if you have not yet overcome the tendency of the mind to wander, it is not advisable for you to perform the *Bloody Sacrifice*.[19] Yet it should not be forgotten that this, and that other art at which we have dared darkly to hint, are the supreme formulae of Practical Magick.

You are also likely to get into trouble over this chapter unless you truly comprehend its meaning.[20]

---

[18] The habitual use of the Lesser Banishing Ritual of the Pentagram (say, thrice daily) for months and years and constant assumption of the God-form of Harpocrates (See Equinox, I, II and Liber 333, cap. XXV for both these) should make the *real circle* i.e. the Aura of the Magus, impregnable.

This Aura should be clean-cut, resilient, radiant, iridescent, brilliant, glittering. "A soap-bubble of razor-steel, streaming with light from within" is my first attempt at description; and is not bad, despite its incongruities: P.

"FRATER PERDURABO on the one occasion on which I was able to see Him as He really appears, was brighter than the Sun at noon. I fell instantly to the floor in a swoon which lasted several hours, during which I was initiated." Soror A.:. Cf. Rev. I, I2-17.

[19] The whole idea of the word Sacrifice, as commonly understood, rests upon an error and superstition, and is unscientific, besides being metaphysically false. The law of Thelema has totally changed the Point of View as to this matter. Unless you have thoroughly assimilated the Formula of Horus, it is absolutely unsafe to meddle with this type of Magick. Let the young Magician reflect upon the Conservation of Matter and of Energy.

[20] There is a traditional saying that whenever an Adept seems to have made a straightforward, comprehensible statement, then is it most certain that He means something entirely different. The Truth is nevertheless clearly set forth in His Words: it is His simplicity that baffles the unworthy. I have chosen the expressions in this Chapter in such a way that it is likely to mislead those magicians who allow selfish interests to cloud their intelligence, but to give useful hints to such as are bound by the proper Oaths to devote their powers to legitimate ends. "Thou hast no right but to do thy will." "It is a lie, this folly against self." The radical error of all uninitiates is that they define "self" as irreconcilably opposed to "not-self." Each element of oneself is, on the contrary, sterile and without meaning, until it fulfils itself, by "love under will", in its counterpart in the Macrocosm. To separate oneself from others is to destroy oneself; the way to realize and to extend oneself is to lose that self—its sense of separateness—in the other. Thus: Child plus food: this does not preserve

Psychopathology Of Sex And Religion

Aleister Crowley—Often called the "Wickedest Man In The World"

---

one at the expense of the other; it "destroys" or rather changes both in order to fulfil both in the result of the operation—a grown man. It is in fact impossible to preserve anything as it is by positive action upon it. Its integrity demands inaction; and inaction, resistance to change, is stagnation, death and dissolution due to the internal putrefaction of the starved elements.

CHAPTER TWENTY FOUR

ENERGIZED ENTHUSIASM

The following essay is probably the most explicit work on Sex Magick that Crowley wrote for public consumption. Written in the Spring of 1912 when he was "hovering between London and Paris," it was published in Equinox Vol. I no.9.

There has been much speculation over the years as to whether the ceremony described below did indeed take place or if it was purely a creation of Crowley's rich imagination. His reference to the Royal Arch and Rose-Croix degrees of Freemasonry intimates that the group would have been a highly irregular branch of Masonry or perhaps Ordo Templi Orientis. Although some elements of the following ceremony are similar to the Mass of the Gnostic Catholic Church (the primary public ceremony of the O.T.O.) and Crowley was very actively involved in the O.T.O. in 1912, it is obvious that it is not the "Mass" as celebrated by the O.T.O.

Historically "true" or not Energized Enthusiasm remains one of the clearest expositions of the underlying theory of Sex Magick and an excellent, if idealized, example of its execution for public worship. We include it in its entirety.

LIBER DCCCXI

ENERGIZED ENTHUSIASM
BY ALEISTER CROWLEY

A NOTE ON THEURGY
I

I A O the supreme One of the Gnostics, the true God, is the Lord of this work. Let us therefore invoke Him by that name which the Companions of the Royal Arch blaspheme to aid us in the essay to declare the means which He has bestowed upon us!

II

The divine consciousness which is reflected and refracted in the works of Genius feeds upon a certain secretion, as I believe. This secretion is analogous to semen, but not identical with it. There are but few men and fewer women, those women being invariably androgyny, who possess it at any time in any quantity.

So closely is this secretion connected with the sexual economy that it appears to me at times as if it might be a by-product of that process which generates semen. That some form of this doctrine has been generally accepted is shown in the prohibitions of all religions. Sanctity has been assumed to depend on chastity, and chastity has nearly always been interpreted as abstinence. But I doubt whether the relation is so simple as this would imply; for example, I find in myself that manifestations of mental creative force always concur with some abnormal condition of the physical powers of generation. But it is not the case that long periods of chastity, on the one hand, or excess of orgies, on the other, are favourable to its manifestation or even to its formation.

I know myself, and in me it is extremely strong; its results are astounding.

For example, I wrote *Tannhauser,* complete from conception to execution, in sixty-seven consecutive hours. I was unconscious of the fall of nights and days, even after stopping; nor was there any reaction of fatigue. This work was written when I was twenty-four years old, immediately on the completion of an orgie which would normally have tired me out.

Often and often have I noticed that sexual satisfaction so-called has left me dissatisfied and unfatigued, and let loose the floods of verse which have disgraced my career.

Yet, on the contrary, a period of chastity has sometimes fortified me for a great outburst. This is far from being invariably the case. At the conclusion of the K2 expedition, after five months of chastity, I did no work whatever, barring very few odd lyrics, for months afterwards.

I may mention the year 1911. At this time I was living, in excellent good health, with the woman whom I loved. Her health was, however, variable, and we were both constantly worried.

The weather was continuously fine and hot. For a period of about three months I hardly missed a morning; always on waking I burst out with a new idea which had to be written down.

The total energy of my being was very high. My weight was 10 stone 8lb., which had been my fighting weight when I was ten years younger. We walked some twenty miles daily through hilly forest.

The actual amount of MSS. written at this time is astounding; their variety is even more so; of their excellence I will not speak.

Here is a rough list from memory; it is far from exhaustive:

(1) Some dozen books of A∴A∴ instruction, including *Liber Astarte,* and *The Temple of Solomon the King* for *The Equinox,* VII.

(2) Short Stories:	"The Woodcutter" "His Secret Sin"
(3) Plays:	*His Majesty's Fiddler*
	Elder Eel
	Adonis and *The Ghouls* {written straight off, one after the other}
	Mortadello
(4) Poems:	"The Sevenfold Sacrament"
	"A Birthday"

(5) Fundamentals of the Greek Qabalah (involving the collection and analysis of several thousand words).

I think this phenomenon is unique in the history of literature.

I may further refer to my second journey to Algeria, where my sexual life, though fairly full, had been unsatisfactory.

On quitting Biskra, I was so full of ideas that I had to get off the train at El-Kantara, where I wrote "The Scorpion." Five or six poems were written on the way to Paris; "The Ordeal of Ida Pendragon" during my twentyfour hours' stay in Paris, and "Snowstorm" and "The Electric Silence" immediately on my return to England.

To sum up, I can always trace a connection between my sexual condition and the condition of artistic creation, which is so close as to approach identity, and yet so loose that I cannot predicate a single important proposition.

It is these considerations which give me pain when I am reproached by the ignorant with wishing to produce genius mechanically. I may fail, but my failure is a thousand times greater than their utmost success.

I shall therefore base my remarks not so much on the observations which I have myself made, and the experiments which I have tried, as on the accepted classical methods of producing that energized enthusiasm which is the lever that moves God.

III

The Greeks say that there are three methods of discharging the genial secretion of which I have spoken. They thought perhaps that their methods tended to secrete it, but this I do not believe altogether, or without a qualm. For the manifestation of force implies force, and this force must have come from somewhere. Easier I find it to say "subconsciousness" and "secretion" than to postulate an external reservoir, to extend my connotation of "man" than to invent " God."

However, parsimony apart, I find it in my experience that it is useless to flog a tired horse. There are times when I am absolutely bereft of even one drop of this elixir. Nothing will restore it, neither rest in bed, nor drugs, nor exercise. On the other hand, sometimes when after a severe spell of work I have been dropping with physical fatigue, perhaps sprawling on the floor, too tired to move hand or foot, the occurrence of an idea has restored me to perfect intensity of energy, and the working out of the idea has actually got rid of the aforesaid physical fatigue, although it involved a great additional labour.

Exactly parallel (nowhere meeting) is the case of mania. A madman may struggle against six trained athletes for hours, and show no sign of fatigue. Then he will suddenly collapse, but at a second's notice from the irritable idea will resume the struggle as fresh as ever. Until we discovered "unconscious muscular action" and its effects, it was rational to suppose such a man "possessed of a devil"; and the difference between the madman and the genius is not in the quantity but in the quality of their work. Genius is organized, madness chaotic. Often the organization of genius is on original lines, and ill-balanced and ignorant medicine-men mistake it for disorder. Time has shown that Whistler and Gauguin "kept rules" as well as the masters whom they were supposed to be upsetting.

IV

The Greeks say that there are three methods of discharging the Leyden Jar of Genius. These three methods they assign to three Gods.

These three Gods are Dionysus, Apollo, Aphrodite. In English: wine, woman and song.

Now it would be a great mistake to imagine that the Greeks were recommending a visit to a brothel. As well condemn the High Mass at St Peter's on the strength of having witnessed a Protestant revival meeting. Disorder is always a parody of order, because there is no archetypal disorder that it might resemble. Owen Seaman can parody a poet; nobody can parody Owen Seaman. A critic is a bundle of impressions; there is no ego behind it. All photographs are essentially alike; the works of all good painters essentially differ.

Some writers suppose that in the ancient rites of Eleusis the High Priest publicly copulated with the High Priestess. Were this so, it would be no more "indecent" than it is "blasphemous" for the priest to make bread and wine into the body and blood of God.

True, the Protestants say that it is blasphemous; but a Protestant is one to whom all things sacred are profane, whose mind being all filth can see nothing in the sexual act but a crime or a jest, whose only facial gestures are the sneer and the leer.

Protestantism is the excrement of human thought, and accordingly in Protestant countries art, if it exist at all, only exists to revolt. Let us return from this unsavoury allusion to our consideration of the methods of the Greeks.

V

Agree then that it does not follow from the fact that wine, woman and song make the sailor's tavern that these ingredients must necessarily concoct a hell-broth.

There are some people so simple as to think that, when they have proved the religious instinct to be a mere efflorescence of the sex-instinct, they have destroyed religion.

We should rather consider that the sailor's tavern gives him his only glimpse of heaven, just as the destructive criticism of the phallicists has only proved sex to be a sacrament. Consciousness, says the materialist, axe in hand, is a function of the brain. He has only re-formulated the old saying, "Your bodies are the temples of the Holy Ghost."!

Now sex is justly hallowed in this sense, that it is the eternal fire of the race. Huxley admitted that "some of the lower animalculae are in a sense immortal," because they go on reproducing eternally by fission, and however often you divide x by 2 there is always something left. But he never seems to have seen that mankind is immortal in exactly the same sense, and goes on reproducing itself with similar characteristics through the ages, changed by circumstance indeed, but always identical in itself. But the spiritual flower of this process is that at the moment of discharge a physical ecstasy occurs, a spasm analogous to the mental spasm which meditation gives. And further, in the sacramental and ceremonial use of the sexual act, the divine consciousness may be attained.

VI

The sexual act being then a sacrament, it remains to consider in what respect this limits the employment of the organs.

First, it is obviously legitimate to employ them for their natural physical purpose. But if it be allowable to use them ceremonially for a religious purpose, we shall find the act hedged about with many restrictions.

For in this case the organs become holy. It matters little to mere propagation that men should be vicious; the most debauched roué might and almost certainly would beget more healthy children than a semi-sexed prude. So the so-called "moral" restraints are not based on reason; thus they are neglected.

But admit its religious function, and one may at once lay down that the act must not be profaned. It must not be undertaken lightly and foolishly without excuse.

It may be undertaken for the direct object of continuing the race.

It may be undertaken in obedience to real passion; for passion, as its name implies, is rather inspired by a force of divine strength and beauty without the will of the individual, often even against it.

It is the casual or habitual—what Christ called "idle"— use or rather abuse of these forces which constitutes their profanation. It will further be obvious that, if the act in itself is to be the sacrament in a religious ceremony, this act must be accomplished solely for the love of God. All personal considerations must be banished utterly. Just as any priest can perform the miracle of transubstantiation, so can any man, possessing the necessary qualifications, perform this other miracle, whose nature must form the subject of a subsequent discussion.

Personal aims being destroyed, it is *a fortiori* necessary to neglect social and other similar considerations.

Physical strength and beauty are necessary and desirable for aesthetic reasons, the attention of the worshippers being liable to distraction if the celebrants are ugly, deformed, or incompetent. I need hardly emphasize the necessity for the strictest self-control and concentration on their part. As it would be blasphemy to enjoy the gross taste of the wine of the sacrament, so must the celebrant suppress even the minutest manifestation of animal pleasure.

Of the qualifying tests there is no necessity to speak; it is sufficient to say that the adepts have always known how to secure efficiency.

Needless also to insist on a similar quality in the assistants; the sexual excitement must be suppressed and transformed into its religious equivalent.

VII

With these preliminaries settled in order to guard against foreseen criticisms of those Protestants who, God having made them a little lower than the Angels, have made themselves a great deal lower than the beasts by their consistently bestial interpretation of all things human and divine, we may consider first the triune nature of these ancient methods of energizing enthusiasm.

Music has two parts; tone or pitch, and rhythm. The latter quality associates it with the dance, and that part of dancing which is not rhythm is sex. Now that part of sex which is not a form of the dance, animal movement, is intoxication of the soul, which connects it with wine. Further identities will suggest themselves to the student.

By the use of the three methods in one the whole being of man may thus be stimulated.

The music will create a general harmony of the brain, leading it in its own paths; the wine affords a general stimulus of the animal nature; and the sex-excitement elevates the moral nature of the man by its close analogy with the highest ecstasy. It remains, however, always for him to make the final transmutation. Unless he have the special secretion which I have postulated, the result will be commonplace.

So consonant is this system with the nature of man that it is exactly parodied and profaned not only in the sailor's tavern, but in the Society ball. Here, for the lowest natures the result is drunkenness, disease and death; for the middle natures a gradual blunting of the finer feelings; for the higher, an exhilaration amounting at the best to the foundation of a life-long love.

If these Society "rites" are properly performed, there should be no exhaustion. After a ball, one should feel the need of a long walk in the young morning air. The weariness or boredom, the headache or somnolence, are Nature's warnings.

VIII

Now the purpose of such a ball, the moral attitude on entering, seems to me to be of supreme importance. If you go with the idea of killing time, you are rather killing yourself. Baudelaire speaks of the first period of love when the boy kisses the trees of the wood, rather than kiss nothing. At the age of thirty-six I found myself at Pompeii, passionately kissing that great grave statue of a woman that stands in the avenue of the tombs. Even now, as I wake in the morning, I sometimes fall to kissing my own arms.

It is with such a feeling that one should go to a ball, and with such a feeling intensified, purified and exalted, that one should leave it.

If this be so, how much more if one go with the direct religious purpose burning in one's whole being! Beethoven roaring at the sunrise is no strange spectacle to me, who shout with joy and wonder, when I understand (without which one cannot really be said ever to see) a blade of grass. I fall upon my knees in speechless adoration at the moon; I hide my eyes in holy awe from a good Van Gogh.

Imagine then a ball in which the music is the choir celestial, the wine the wine of the Graal, or that of the Sabbath of the Adepts, and one's partner the Infinite and Eternal One, the True and Living God Most High!

Go even to a common ball—the Moulin de la Galette will serve even the least of my magicians—with your whole soul aflame within you, and your whole will concentrated on these transubstantiations, and tell me what miracle takes place!

It is the hate of, the distaste for, life that sends one to the ball when one is old; when one is young one is on springs until the hour falls; but the love of God, which is the only true love, diminishes not with age; it grows deeper and intenser with every satisfaction. It seems as if in the noblest men this secretion constantly increases—which certainly suggests an external reservoir—so that age loses all its bitterness. We find "Brother Lawrence," Nicholas Herman of Lorraine, at the age of eighty in continuous enjoyment of union with God. Buddha at an equal age would run up and down the Eight High Trances like an acrobat on a ladder; stories not too dissimilar are told of Bishop Berkeley. Many persons have not attained union at all until middle age, and then have rarely lost it.

It is true that genius in the ordinary sense of the word has nearly always showed itself in the young. Perhaps we should regard such cases as Nicholas Herman as cases of acquired genius.

Now I am certainly of opinion that genius can be acquired, or, in the alternative, that it is an almost universal possession. Its rarity may be attributed to the crushing influence of a corrupted society. It is rare to meet a youth without high ideals, generous thoughts, a sense of holiness, of his own importance, which, being interpreted, is, of his own identity with God. Three years in the world, and he is a bank clerk or even a government official. Only those who intuitively understand from early boyhood that they must stand out, and who have the incredible courage and endurance to do so in face of all that tyranny, callousness, and the scorn of inferiors can do; only these arrive at manhood uncontaminated.

Every serious or spiritual thought is made a jest; poets are thought "soft" and "cowardly," apparently because they are the only boys with a will of their own and courage to hold out against the whole school, boys and masters in league as once were Pilate and Herod; honour is replaced by expediency, holiness by hypocrisy.

Even where we find thoroughly good seed sprouting in favourable ground, too often is there a frittering away of the forces. Facile encouragement of a poet or painter is far worse for him than any amount of opposition. Here again the sex question (S.Q. so-called by Tolstoyans, chastity-mongers, nut-fooders, and such who talk and think of nothing else) intrudes its horrid head. I believe that every boy is originally conscious of sex as sacred. But he does not know what it is. With infinite diffidence he asks. The master replies with holy horror; the boy with a low leer, a furtive laugh, perhaps worse.

I am inclined to agree with the Head Master of Eton that paederastic passions among schoolboys "do no harm"; further, I think them the only redeeming feature of sexual life at public schools.

The Hindoos are wiser. At the well-watched hour of puberty the boy is prepared as for a sacrament; he is led to a duly consecrated temple, and there by a wise and holy woman, skilled in the art, and devoted to this end, he is initiated with all solemnity into the mystery of life.

The act is thus declared religious, sacred, impersonal, utterly apart from amorism and eroticism and animalism and sentimentalism and all the other vilenesses that Protestantism has made of it.

The Catholic Church did, I believe, to some extent preserve the Pagan tradition. Marriage is a sacrament[1]. But in the attempt to deprive the act of all accretions which would profane it, the Fathers of the Church added in spite of themselves other accretions which profaned it more. They tied it to property and inheritance. They wished it to serve both God and Mammon.

Rightly restraining the priest, who should employ his whole energy in the miracle of the Mass, they found their counsel a counsel of perfection. The magical tradition was in part lost; the priest could not do what was expected of him, and the unexpended portion of his energy turned sour.

Hence the thoughts of priests, like the thoughts of modern faddists, revolved eternally around the S.Q.

A special and Secret Mass, a Mass of the Holy Ghost, a Mass of the Mystery of the Incarnation, to be performed at stated intervals, might have saved both monks and nuns, and given the Church eternal dominion of the world.

IX

To return. The rarity of genius is in great part due to the destruction of its young. Even as in physical life that is a favoured plant one of whose thousand seeds ever shoots forth a blade, so do conditions kill all but the strongest sons of genius.

But just as rabbits increased apace in Australia, where even a missionary has been known to beget ninety children in two years, so shall we be able to breed genius if we can find the conditions which hamper it, and remove them.

The obvious practical step to take is to restore the rites of Bacchus, Aphrodite and Apollo to their proper place. They should not be open to every one, and manhood should be the reward of ordeal and initiation.

---

[1] Of course there has been a school of devilish ananders that has held the act in itself to be "wicked." Of such blasphemers of Nature let no further word be said.

Psychopathology Of Sex And Religion

The physical tests should be severe, and weaklings should be killed out rather than artificially preserved. The same remark applies to intellectual tests. But such tests should be as wide as possible. I was an absolute duffer at school in all forms of athletics and games, because I despised them. I held, and still hold, numerous mountaineering world's records. Similarly, examinations fail to test intelligence. Cecil Rhodes refused to employ any man with a University degree. That such degrees lead to honour in England is a sign of England's decay, though even in England they are usually the stepping stones to clerical idleness or pedagogic slavery.

Such is a dotted outline of the picture that I wish to draw. If the power to possess property depended on a man's competence, and his perception of real values, a new aristocracy would at once be created, and the deadly fact that social consideration varies with the power of purchasing champagne would cease to be a fact. Our pluto-hetairo-politicocracy would fall in a day.

But I am only too well aware that such a picture is not likely to be painted. We can then only work patiently and in secret. We must select suitable material and train it in utmost reverence to these three master-methods, or aiding the soul in its genial orgasm

This reverent attitude is of an importance which I cannot over-rate. Normal people find normal relief from any general or special excitement in the sexual act.

Commander Marston, R.N., whose experiments in the effect of the tom-tom on the married Englishwoman are classical and conclusive, has admirably described how the vague unrest which she at first shows gradually assumes the sexual form, and culminates, if allowed to do so, in shameless masturbation or indecent advances. But this is a natural corollary of the proposition that married Englishwomen are usually unacquainted with sexual satisfaction. Their desires are constantly stimulated by brutal and ignorant husbands, and never gratified. This fact again accounts for the amazing prevalence of Sapphism in London Society.

The Hindus warn their pupils against the dangers of breathing exercises. Indeed the slightest laxness in moral or physical tissues may cause the energy accumulated by the practice to discharge itself by involuntary emission. I have known this happen in my own experience.

It is then of the utmost importance to realize that the relief of the tension is to be found in what the Hebrews and the Greeks called prophesying, and which is better when organized into art. The disorderly discharge is mere waste, a wilderness of howlings; the orderly discharge is a "Prometheus unbound," or a "L'age d'airain," according to the special aptitudes of the enthused person. But it must be remembered that special aptitudes are very easy to acquire if the driving force of enthusiasm be great. If you cannot keep the rules of others, you make rules of your own. One set turns out in the long run to be just as good as another.

Henri Rousseau, the douanier, was laughed at all his life. I laughed as heartily as the rest; though, almost despite myself, I kept on saying (as the phrase goes) "that I felt something; couldn't say what."

The moment it occurred to somebody to put up all his paintings in one room by themselves, it was instantly apparent that his *naiveté* was the simplicity of a Master.

Let no one then imagine that I fail to perceive or underestimate the dangers of employing these methods. The occurrence even of so simple a matter as fatigue might change a Las Meninas into a stupid sexual crisis.

It will be necessary for most Englishmen to emulate the self-control of the Arabs and Hindus, whose ideal is to deflower the greatest possible number of virgins—eighty is considered a fairly good performance—without completing the act.

It is, indeed, of the first importance for the celebrant in any phallic rite to be able to complete the act without even once allowing a sexual or sensual thought to invade his mind. The mind must be as absolutely detached from one's own body as it is from another person's.

XI

Of musical instruments few are suitable. The human voice is the best, and the only one which can be usefully employed in chorus. Anything like an orchestra implies infinite rehearsal, and introduces an atmosphere of artificiality. The organ is a worthy solo instrument, and is an orchestra in itself, while its tone and associations favour the religious idea.

The violin is the most useful of all, for its every mood expresses the hunger for the infinite, and yet it is so mobile that it has a greater emotional range than any of its competitors. Accompaniment must be dispensed with, unless a harpist be available.

The harmonium is a horrible instrument, if only because of its associations; and the piano is like unto it, although, if unseen and played by a Paderewski, it would serve.

The trumpet and the bell are excellent, to startle, at the crises of a ceremony.

Hot, drubbing, passionate, in a different class of ceremony, a class more intense and direct, but on the whole less exalted, the tom-tom stands alone. It combines well with the practice of mantra, and is the best accompaniment for any sacred dance.

XII

Of sacred dances the most practical for a gathering is the seated dance. One sits cross-legged on the floor, and sways to and fro from the hips in time with the mantra. A solo or duet of dancers as a spectacle rather distracts from this exercise. I would suggest a very small and very brilliant light on the floor in the middle of the room. Such a room is best floored with mosaic marble; an ordinary Freemason's Lodge carpet is not a bad thing.

The eyes, if they see anything at all, see then only the rhythmical or mechanical squares leading in perspective to the simple unwinking light.

The swinging of the body with the mantra (which has a habit of rising and falling as if of its own accord in a very weird way) becomes more accentuated; ultimately a curiously spasmodic stage occurs, and then the consciousness flickers and goes out; perhaps breaks through into the divine consciousness, perhaps is merely recalled to itself by some variable in external impression.

The above is a very simple description of a very simple and earnest form of ceremony, based entirely upon rhythm.

It is very easy to prepare, and its results are usually very encouraging for the beginner.

XIII

Wine being a mocker and strong drink raging, its use is more likely to lead to trouble than mere music.

One essential difficulty is dosage. One needs exactly enough; and, as Blake points out, one can only tell what is enough by taking too much. For each man the dose varies enormously; so does it for the same man at different times.

The ceremonial escape from this is to have a noiseless attendant to bear the bowl of libation, and present it to each in turn, at frequent intervals. Small doses should be drunk, and the bowl passed on, taken as the worshipper deems advisable. Yet the cup-bearer should be an initiate, and use his own discretion before presenting the bowl. The slightest sign that intoxication is mastering the man should be a sign to him to pass that man. This practice can be easily fitted to the ceremony previously described.

If desired, instead of wine, the elixir introduced by me to Europe may be employed. But its results, if used in this way, have not as yet been thoroughly studied. It is my immediate purpose to repair this neglect.

XIV

The sexual excitement, which must complete the harmony of method, offers a more difficult problem.

It is exceptionally desirable that the actual bodily movements involved should be decorous in the highest sense, and many people are so ill-trained that they will be unable to regard such a ceremony with any but critical or lascivious eyes; either would be fatal to all the good already done. It is presumably better to wait until all present are greatly exalted before risking a profanation.

It is not desirable, in my opinion, that the ordinary worshippers should celebrate in public.

The sacrifice should be single.

Whether or no...

XV

Thus far had I written when the distinguished poet, whose conversation with me upon the Mysteries had incited me to jot down these few rough notes, knocked at my door. I told him that I was at work on the ideas suggested by him, and that—well, I was rather stuck. He asked permission to glance at the MS. (for he reads English fluently, though speaking but a few words), and having done so, kindled and said: "If you come with me now, we will finish your essay." Glad enough of any excuse to stop working, the more plausible the better, I hastened to take down my coat and hat.

"By the way," he remarked in the automobile, "I take it that you do not mind giving me the Word of Rose Croix." Surprised, I exchanged the secrets of I.N.R.I. with him. "And now, very excellent and perfect Prince," he said, "what follows is under this seal." And he gave me the most solemn of all Masonic tokens. "You are about," said he, "to compare your ideal with our real."

He touched a bell. The automobile stopped, and we got out. He dismissed the chauffeur. "Come," he said, "we have a brisk half-mile." We walked through thick woods to an old house, where we were greeted in silence by a gentleman who, though in court dress, wore a very "practicable" sword. On satisfying him, we were passed through a corridor to an anteroom, where another armed guardian awaited us. He, after a further examination, proceeded to offer me a court dress, the insignia of a Sovereign Prince of Rose Croix, and a garter and mantle, the former of green silk, the latter of green velvet, and lined with cerise silk. "It is a low mass," whispered the guardian. In this anteroom were three or four others, both ladies and gentlemen, busily robing.

In a third room we found a procession formed, and joined it. There were twenty-six of us in all. Passing a final guardian we reached the chapel itself, at whose entrance stood a young man and a young woman, both dressed in simple robes of white silk embroidered with gold, red and blue. The former bore a torch of resinous wood, the latter sprayed us as we passed with attar of roses from a cup.

The room in which we now were had at one time been a chapel; so much its shape declared. But the high altar was covered with a cloth that displayed the Rose and Cross, while above it were ranged seven candelabra, each of seven branches.

The stalls had been retained; and at each knight's hand burned a taper of rose-coloured wax, and a bouquet of roses was before him.

In the centre of the nave was a great cross—a "calvary cross of ten squares," measuring, say, six feet by five painted in red upon a white board, at whose edge were rings through which passed gilt staves. At each corner was a banner, bearing lion, bull, eagle and man, and from the top of their staves sprang a canopy of blue, wherein were figured in gold the twelve emblems of the Zodiac.

Knights and Dames being installed, suddenly a bell tinkled in the architrave. Instantly all rose. The doors opened at a trumpet peal from without, and a herald advanced, followed by the High Priest and Priestess.

The High Priest was a man of nearly sixty years, if I may judge by the white beard; but he walked with the springy yet assured step of the thirties. The High Priestess, a proud, tall sombre woman of perhaps thirty summers, walked by his side, their hands raised and touching as in the minuet. Their trains were borne by the two youths who had admitted us.

All this while an unseen organ played an Introit.

This ceased as they took their places at the altar. They faced West, waiting.

On the closing of the doors the armed guard, who was clothed in a scarlet robe instead of green, drew his sword, and went up and down the aisle, chanting exorcisms and swinging the great sword. All present drew their swords and faced outward, holding the points in front of them. This part of the ceremony appeared interminable. When it was over the girl and boy reappeared; bearing, the one a bowl, the other a censer. Singing some litany or other, apparently in Greek, though I could not catch the words, they purified and consecrated the chapel.

Now the High Priest and High Priestess began a litany in rhythmic lines of equal length. At each third response they touched hands in a peculiar manner; at each seventh they kissed. The twenty-first was a complete embrace. The bell tinkled in the architrave; and they parted. The High Priest then took from the altar a flask curiously shaped to imitate a phallus. The High Priestess knelt and presented a boat-shaped cup of gold. He knelt opposite her, and did not pour from the flask.

Now the Knights and Dames began a long litany; first a Dame in treble, then a Knight in bass, then a response in chorus of all present with the organ. This Chorus was:
EVOE HO, IACCHE! EPELTHON, EPELTHON, EVOE, IAO!

Again and again it rose and fell. Towards its close, whether by "stage effect" or no I could not swear, the light over the altar grew rosy, then purple. The High Priest sharply and suddenly threw up his hand; instant silence.

He now poured out the wine from the flask. The High Priestess gave it to the girl attendant, who bore it to all present.

This was no ordinary wine. It has been said of vodka that it looks like water and tastes like fire. With this wine the reverse is the case. It was of a rich fiery gold in which flames of light danced and shook, but its taste was limpid and pure like fresh spring water. No sooner had I drunk of it, however, than I began to tremble. It was a most astonishing sensation; I can imagine a man feel thus as he awaits his executioner, when he has passed through fear, and is all excitement.

I looked down my stall, and saw that each was similarly affected. During the libation the High Priestess sang a hymn, again in Greek. This time I recognized the words; they were those of an ancient Ode to Aphrodite.

The boy attendant now descended to the red cross, stooped and kissed it; then he danced upon it in such a way that he seemed to be tracing the patterns of a marvellous rose of gold, for the percussion caused a shower of bright dust to fall from the canopy. Meanwhile the litany (different words, but the same chorus) began again. This time it was a duet between the High Priest and Priestess. At each chorus Knights and Dames bowed low. The girl moved round continuously, and the bowl passed.

This ended in the exhaustion of the boy, who fell fainting on the cross. The girl immediately took the bowl and put it to his lips. Then she raised him, and, with the assistance of the Guardian of the Sanctuary, led him out of the chapel.

The bell again tinkled in the architrave.

The herald blew a fanfare.

The High Priest and High Priestess moved stately to each other and embraced, in the act unloosing the heavy golden robes which they wore. These fell, twin lakes of gold. I now saw her dressed in a garment of white watered silk, lined throughout (as it appeared later) with ermine.

The High Priest's vestment was an elaborate embroidery of every colour, harmonized by exquisite yet robust art. He wore also a breastplate corresponding to the canopy; a sculptured "beast" at each corner in gold, while the twelve signs of the Zodiac were symbolized by the stones of the breastplate.

The bell tinkled yet again, and the herald again sounded his trumpet. The celebrants moved hand in hand down the nave while the organ thundered forth its solemn harmonies.

All the Knights and Dames rose and gave the secret sign of the Rose Croix.

It was at this part of the ceremony that things began to happen to me. I became suddenly aware that my body had lost both weight and tactile sensibility. My consciousness seemed to be situated no longer in my body. I "mistook myself," if I may use the phrase, for one of the stars in the canopy.

In this way I missed seeing the celebrants actually approach the cross. The bell tinkled again; I came back to myself, and then I saw that the High Priestess, standing at the foot of the cross, had thrown her robe over it, so that the cross was no longer visible. There was only a board covered with ermine. She was now naked but for her coloured and jewelled head-dress and the heavy torque of gold about her neck, and the armlets and anklets that matched it. She began to sing in a soft strange tongue, so low and smoothly that in my partial bewilderment I could not hear all; but I caught a few words, Io Pan! Io Pan! and a phrase in which the words Iao Sabao ended emphatically a sentence in which I caught the words Eros, Thelema and Sebazo.

While she did this she unloosed the breastplate and gave it to the girl attendant. The robe followed; I saw that they were naked and unashamed. For the first time there was absolute silence.

Now, from an hundred jets surrounding the board poured forth a perfumed purple smoke. The world was wrapt in a

fond gauze of mist, sacred as the clouds upon the mountains.
Then at a signal given by the High Priest, the bell tinkled once more. The celebrants stretched out their arms in the form of a cross, interlacing their fingers. Slowly they revolved through three circles and a half. She then laid him down upon the cross, and took her own appointed place.
The organ now again rolled forth its solemn music.
I was lost to everything. Only this I saw, that the celebrants made no expected motion. The movements were extremely small and yet extremely strong.
This must have continued for a great length of time. To me it seemed as if eternity itself could not contain the variety and depth of my experiences. Tongue nor pen could record them; and yet I am fain to attempt the impossible.

1. I was, certainly and undoubtedly, the star in the canopy. This star was an incomprehensibly enormous world of pure flame.
2. I suddenly realized that the star was of no size whatever. It was not that the star shrank, but that it (= I) became suddenly conscious of infinite space.
3. An explosion took place. I was in consequence a point of light, infinitely small, yet infinitely bright, and this point was *without position*.
4. Consequently this point was ubiquitous, and there was a feeling of infinite bewilderment, blinded after a very long time by a gush of infinite rapture. (I use the word "blinded" as if under constraint; I should have preferred to use the words "blotted out" or "overwhelmed" or "illuminated.")
5. This infinite fullness—I have not described it as such, but it was that—was suddenly changed into a feeling of infinite emptiness, which became conscious as a yearning.
6. These two feelings began to alternate, always with suddenness, and without in any way overlapping, with great rapidity.
7. This alternation must have occurred fifty times—I had rather have said an hundred.

8. The two feelings suddenly became one. Again the word explosion is the only one that gives any idea of it.

9. I now seemed to be conscious of everything at once, that it was at the same time *one* and *many*. I say "at once," that is, I was not successively all things, but instantaneously.

10. This being, if I may call it being, seemed to drop into an infinite abyss of Nothing.

11. While this "falling" lasted, the bell suddenly tinkled three times. I instantly became my normal self, yet with a constant awareness, which has never left me to this hour, that the truth of the matter is not this normal "I" but "That" which is still dropping into Nothing. I am assured by those who know that I may be able to take up the thread if I attend another ceremony.

The tinkle died away. The girl attendant ran quickly forward and folded the ermine over the celebrants. The herald blew a fanfare, and the Knights and Dames left their stalls. Advancing to the board, we took hold of the gilded carrying poles, and followed the herald in procession out of the chapel, bearing the litter to a small sidechapel leading out of the middle anteroom, where we left it, the guard closing the doors.

In silence we disrobed, and left the house. About a mile through the woods we found my friend's automobile waiting.

I asked him, if that was a low mass, might I not be permitted to witness a High Mass?

"Perhaps," he answered with a curious smile, "if all they tell of you is true."

In the meanwhile he permitted me to describe the ceremony and its results as faithfully as I was able, charging me only to give no indication of the city near which it took place.

I am willing to indicate to initiates of the Rose Croix degree of Masonry under proper charter from the genuine authorities (for there are spurious Masons working under a forged charter) the address of a person willing to consider their fitness to affiliate to a Chapter practising similar rites.

XVI

I consider it supererogatory to continue my essay on the Mysteries and my analysis of *Energized Enthusiasm*.

CHAPTER TWENTY FIVE

THE SECRET OF THE HOLY GRAAL

The Quest for the **Holy Graal** has occupied the imagination of the Western mind since the Middle Ages.

In the Romance languages San Graal means Holy Graal and Sang Real means Blood Royal (or Holy Blood). This Blood is the Life of the Magician both allegorically and in actuality. Obviously, in a ritual of Sex Magick, Holy Blood could be interpreted as the semen of the Priest and the Holy Graal as the vagina and womb of the Priestess.

The imagery of this work deals with the Second Great Magical Crisis, the Crossing of the Abyss. (The First Great Magical Event being the attainment of the Knowledge and Conversation of the Holy Guardian Angel, enlightenment or spiritual awakening.)

Metaphorically speaking The Abyss can be considered the anti-dimensional wasteland that separates Absolute Reality from Relative Existence; the One from the Many, God from Creation. No idea can exist above the Abyss that does not contain and reconcile its own opposite.

It is for this reason, to those below the abyss, the imagery of the following work appears averse, blasphemous and "evil" for we are viewing it from the "below-the-Abyss" point of view, attempting to intellectually comprehend the incomprehensible. The Divine images pass down through the lens of the Abyss and are turned up-side down and inside out.

The Initiation of Crossing the Abyss demands the absolute annihilation of not only the Ego but also of all the perceived *qualities* of Self. The Magician is said to pour out completely his Life's Blood in this experience. Keeping back one drop, one thought, insures utter failure and a spiritual catastrophe of unimaginable proportions.

On the Qabalistic diagram called the Tree of Life, the Abyss is located between the Fourth Sephirah, Chesed and the Third Sephirah, Binah. Binah is the abode of the Goddess Babalon the Great, who is symbolic of the Universal Life.

She is called the **Scarlet Woman** because she passionately offers herself indiscriminately to All. (She can never be taken nor can she be bribed, bought or given away.) She is **Babalon**, **Bab** (the Gate) **Al** (God) **On** (Being), The Gate of the God of Being. She is the Great Whore who offers herself to the **ALL**—the Divine Totality who alone can fill her divine and infinite vessel.

In Her "Adulteries," She shamelessly receives the Life (Blood) of the entire universe in Her Holy Graal, and She becomes "drunk." As She resides above the Abyss, where all opposites are reconciled, we call her the Mother of Abominations. Her "children" are neither (and both) Good, Evil, Holy *and* Abominable.

Her lover is the Lord Chaos, the Beast who resides in the Second Sephirah, Chokmah. He is called Chaos for He is the Creator of the Duality that initially destroyed the profound simplicity of the ONE.

When Babalon has gathered the "Blood of the Saints" in Her Great Cup, she delivers it to Her Lord Chaos and He too drinks and becomes "awakened" to the ultimate reality of the ONE. Only through the union of these two Divinities can the First Sephirah be achieved and the Magician dissolve into Godhead.

ח[1]

LIBER CHETH
VEL
VALLUM ABIEGNI[2]
SUB FIGURA
CLVI[3]

BY
ALEISTER CROWLEY

1. This is the secret of the Holy Graal, that is the sacred vessel of our Lady the Scarlet Woman, Babalon the Mother of Abominations, the bride of Chaos, that rideth upon our Lord the Beast.
2. Thou shalt drain out thy blood that is thy life into the golden cup of her fornication.
3. Thou shalt mingle thy life with the universal life. Thou shalt keep not back one drop.
4. Then shall thy brain be dumb, and thy heart beat no more, and all thy life shall go from thee, and thou shalt be cast out upon the midden, and the birds of the air shall feast upon thy flesh, and thy bones shall whiten in the sun.
5. Then shall the winds gather themselves together, and bear thee up as it were a little heap of dust in a sheet that hath four corners, and they shall give it unto the guardians of the abyss.
6. And because there is no life therein, the guardians of the abyss shall bid the angels of the winds pass by. And the

---

[1] The Hebrew letter Cheth, is attributed to the Tarot card, The Chariot. It is the Charioteer who bears and is the Guardian of the Holy Graal.
  Spelled in full ח י ת , it adds to 418 the number of the magical word ABRAHADABRA which symbolizes the union of the Macrocosm and the Microcosm, the Great work accomplished.

[2] The Wall of Abiegnus (the Sacred Mountain of the Rosicrucians)

[3] 156 the numeration of the Goddess Babalon

Taboo: The Ecstasy Of Evil

angels shall lay thy dust in the City of Pyramids, and the name thereof shall be no more.

7. Now therefore that thou mayest achieve this ritual of the Holy Graal, do thou divest thyself of all thy goods.

8. Thou hast wealth; give it unto them that have need thereof, yet no desire toward it.

9. Thou hast health; slay thyself in the fervour of thine abandonment unto our Lady. Let thy flesh hang loose upon thy bones, and thine eyes glare with thy quenchless lust unto the Infinite, with thy passion for the Unknown, for Her that is beyond Knowledge the accursed one.

10. Thou hast love; tear thy mother from thine heart, and spit in the face of thy father. Let thy foot trample the belly of thy wife, and let the babe at her breast be the prey of dogs and vultures.

11. For if thou dost not this with thy will, then shall We do this despite thy will. So that thou attain to the Sacrament of the Graal in the Chapel of Abominations.

12. And behold! if by stealth thou keep unto thyself one thought of thine, then shalt thou be cast out into the abyss for ever; and thou shalt be the lonely one, the eater of dung, the afflicted in the Day of Be-With-Us.

13. Yea! verily this is the Truth, this is the Truth, this is the Truth. Unto thee shall be granted joy and health and wealth and wisdom when thou art no longer thou.

14. Then shall every gain be a new sacrament, and it shall not defile thee; thou shalt revel with the wanton in the market-place, and the virgins shall fling roses upon thee, and the merchants bend their knees and bring thee gold and spices. Also young boys shall pour wonderful wines for thee, and the singers and the dancers shall sing and dance for thee.

15. Yet shalt thou not be therein, for thou shalt be forgotten, dust lost in dust.

16. Nor shall the aeon itself avail thee in this; for from the dust shall a white ash be prepared by Hermes the Invisible.

17. And this is the wrath of God, that these things should be thus.

18. And this is the grace of God, that these things should be thus.

19. Wherefore, I charge you that ye come unto me in the Beginning; for if ye take but one step in this Path, ye must arrive inevitably at the end thereof.

20. This Path is beyond Life and Death; it is also beyond Love but that ye know not, for ye know not Love.

21. And the end thereof is known not even unto Our Lady or to the Beast whereon She rideth; nor unto the Virgin her daughter nor unto Chaos her lawful Lord; but unto the Crowned Child is it known? It is not known if it be Known.

22. Therefore unto Hadit and unto Nuit be they glory in the End and the beginning; yea, in the End and the Beginning.

CHAPTER TWENTY SIX

SEXUAL ALCHEMY

With a literary technique diametrical to that of Aleister Crowley's *Bloody Sacrifice,* Israel Regardie treated the subject of Sex Magick with great tact and a high level of spiritual diplomacy. Chapter Sixteen of his 1932 classic, *The Tree of Life* (Weiser 1988) is a perfect example.

With incredible subtly and in the language of Alchemy, he reveals the theory and operating procedures of one of the most closely guarded secrets of Sex Magick, and, like Crowley, he does it in such a way as to render it completely unintelligible to the average reader.

We have reproduced the essay as re-edited by Regardie and complete with his additional notes. It has never before appeared in print in this form.

As he makes several references to the Y.H.V.H. formula, we have included below a few words on the subject from our book *The Way of the Secret Lover* (New Falcon Publications 1991).

ה ו ה י
(Y H V H)
THE ORIGINAL FOUR LETTER WORD

YHVH, *vulgarly* pronounced Jehovah by the ignorant, a name of God so sacred to Judaism that Jews to this day are forbidden to pronounce it and instead when they see it in print replace it with the word **Adonai.**

This Divine name is referred to as the Tetragrammaton and the four letters represent the totality of the forces and energies of creation divided into four distinct "worlds."

י

Y (Yod)
Represents the highest Spiritual Realm from which all other worlds are born. One could almost describe it as the Will (Wand) of God. This World is called **ATZILUTH** and is designated the **Archetypal World**.

ה

H (Heh)
Represents the **Creative World** where the archetypes of creation (coming down from Atziluth) are impressed into concepts. This World is called **BRIAH** and could be considered the Soul (Cup) of God.

ו

V (Vau)
Represents the **Formative World** where the concepts coming down from Briah are actually formulated into the "blueprints" of what will eventually become the material universe. This World is called **YETZIRAH** and could be viewed as the Divine engineering department, the Mind (Sword) of God.

ה

H (Heh, *final*)
Represents the **Material World**—the phenomenal universe and all the energies, seen and unseen, that comprise it. This World is called **ASSIAH**. What started as the impulse of Atziluth became the concept of Briah that became the "blueprint" of Yetzirah, finally manifests in the fourth world, Assiah (Disk).

Yod is the Father, a **King**. He "weds"
Heh, the Mother his **Queen**
  who gives birth to twins, a boy, and a girl;
Vau, the **Prince** and
Heh (f), the **Princess**

It is easy to see in the above "family story" the mechanics of the descent of Spirit into Matter. The Primal Fire impregnates itself upon Primal Water which becomes the womb for Primal Air and eventually the Primal Earth of the material world.

In the poetic imagery of the Qabalah, humanity is the final **Heh**. Like an enchanted Princess in a fairytale we find ourselves trapped in the material universe far away from our Mother the Queen and our Father the King. Unless we are rescued we will never attain our rightful place on the Throne.

But rescue is *in the cards* for the story does not end here. This family is also the key to our *return* from the material world to that of the Divine.

Heh (f) The **Princess** surrenders herself as lover to
Vau The **Prince** who weds her. She becomes pregnant making her
Heh the **Queen**, making the Prince
Yod the **King**.

The remarkable thing about these two stories is that they are happening eternally at the same time. Just as an alternating current of electricity passes through a wire in both directions simultaneously so too does the "electromagnetic" power of YHVH pass through every level of creation including you and me.

THE MASS OF THE HOLY GHOST

By
Israel Regardie

When commencing to outline and write this book on Magic, it was the firm intention of the writer to elucidate all magical processes as simply and as intelligibly as was both humanly possible and consistent with proper exegetical treatment of a highly difficult and complex subject. Because there has been in the past so much willful obscurity and intentionally misleading matter, it seemed high time to provide a statement which could be utilized once and for all as a clear, definite exposition. The writer hopes that he has kept to this intention throughout, although that is a point of which the reader must be the sole judge. Ambiguity and sometimes deliberate attempt to deceive, through the employment of difficult symbolism and mention of large series of authoritative names, have characterized a number of magical books, thus vitiating whatever value was theirs.

There remains to be outlined in this work one secret formula of Practical Magic of such a tremendous nature—shrouded as it always has been in the past by the glamour of recondite symbols and hidden by heavy veils—that the writer is doubtful as to whether it would be wise or politic to adhere to his original decision. It might, of course, have been omitted from the general contents, but to render this treatise moderately complete so far as the major, though elementary, aspects of the Higher Magic are concerned it was necessary to include it in some form. The method of which it is proposed to speak is so puissant a formula of the Magic of Light, and one so liable to indiscriminate abuse and use in Black Magic, that if a conception of its technique and theory is to be presented at all then the original intent of the writer must be discarded. It will be necessary to resort to the medium of an eloquent symbolism which for centuries has been utilized for the conveyance of these and similar ideas. And the reader must be assured that the symbolism has not been purposely muddled, nor has it been rendered ambiguous, obscure and meaningless. If carefully studied the terms employed will reveal a consistency and a continuity which will disclose to the right people in a quite accurate manner the processes of its technique.

The Mass of the Holy Ghost! Thus is this particular technique named. It is unique in the whole of Magic, for therein are comprehended almost every known form of Theurgic procedure. Simultaneously, it is the quintessence and the synthesis of them all. Among other things it concerns the Magic of Talismans. By this method a living spiritual force is bound into a specific telesmatic substance. Not dead or inert is this telesmata as obtains in the customary ceremonial talismanic evocation; but it is one at once vibrant, dynamic, and containing in germ and potentiality the possibility of all growth and development. In a Very special way, it concerns moreover the formula of the Holy Grail. A golden Chalice of spiritual grace is employed, into which the very essence and life-blood of the Theurgist must be poured for the redemption not of his own soul but that thereby all mankind might be saved. The Eucharist too is implicit, and the Chalice is used as the communion cup, the hallowed contents of which—thaumaturgic and iridescent; the sacramental wine, in short—must be dedicated and consecrated to the service of the Most High. The Oblation to be consumed with the Eucharistic wine is, by this interpretation, the secret essence of both the intoxicated Magician and the supreme God whom he has invoked. In this method also is imputed to a very large degree the alchemical technique, inasmuch as it concerns for the most part the production of the potable Gold, the Stone of the Philosophers, and the Elixir of Life which is Amrita, the Dew of Immortality.

Above all should the reader retain in mind the philosophical formula of the Tetragrammaton which is the method of this Mass. This demonstrates the necessity for a practical acquaintance with the numerical principles of the Holy Qabalah, for the more knowledge one possesses and has systematically classified under the index system of the Tree of Life, the more meaning and significance attaches itself to the Tetragrammaton formula. In the chapter sketching the magical theory of the universe the general implications of the sacred Name were briefly explained in those connections. These ideas should be thoroughly assimilated in relation to the Tree. With that understanding the reader should apply his powers to the symbolic scheme which now follows.

Illustrating one chapter-head in Franz Hartman's *Secret Symbols of the Rosicrucians* is a drawing of a mermaid rising from the sea. To her breasts her hands are held, and there issue therefrom two streams returning into the sea. In explanation of this figure Hartman wrote that "The figure represents the foundation of things and from which all things are born. It is a dual principle of nature; its parents are the Sun and the Moon; it produces water and wine, gold and silver, by the blessing of God. If you torture the Eagle the Lion will become feeble. The 'Eagle's tears' and the 'red blood of the Lion' must meet and mingle. The Eagle and the Lion bathe, eat, and love each other. They will become like the Salamander and become constant in the fire."

Prior to proceeding further with the analysis of aspects of this Operation, I should like to place before the reader a quotation wherein this Mass is repeated at some length, using the conventional nomenclature of alchemy. "I am a goddess for beauty and extraction famous, born out of our proper sea which compasseth the whole earth and is ever restless. Out of my breasts I pour forth milk and blood; boil these two till they are turned into silver and gold. O most excellent subject, out of which all things are generated, though at first sight thou art poison, adorned with the name of the Flying Eagle...Thy parents are the Sun and Moon; in thee there is water and wine, gold also and silver upon earth, that mortal man may rejoice...But consider, O man, what things God bestows upon thee by this means. Torture the Eagle till she weeps and the Lion be weakened and bleed to death. The blood of this Lion incorporated with the tears of the Eagle is the treasure of the earth." This, without doubt, is also in explanation of the figure reproduced by Franz Hartman.

In elaboration of the above, the following principles may be postulated. The Y of the sacred Name in this system is called the Red Lion, and the first H is the White Eagle.

These two letters are conceived to be the representations of two cosmic principles, two rivers of scarlet blood which pour from the breasts of the mermaid into the sea, two distinct ever-flowing streams of life and light and love which proceed eternally from Life itself. In them is the power of touching and communing, making new one the other, without any breaking of the subtle confines of the flowing streams, nor any confusion of substance. Mutually complementary and opposite in nature are they; yet in them is grounded the entirety of existence. All alchemical operations according to authority require two major instruments: "one circular, crystalline vessel, justly proportioned to the quality of its contents" or the Cucurbite, and "one theosophic, cabalistically sealed furnace or Athanor."[1] The Athanor is assigned to the Y, and the Cucurbite is an attribution of the H.

Now although the pure Gold of which mention was made is a homogeneous substance, one and indivisible, dynamic and pregnant with infinite possibility, nevertheless two separate substances are used in its production. These are named the Serpent or the Blood of the Red Lion, and the Tears or the Gluten of the White Eagle. The Serpent is an attribution of the V of Tetragrammaton, and to the last H of that Name the Gluten is allocated. These two substances are the offspring, as it were, of the Lion and the Eagle. The alchemical instruments aforementioned are to be considered as the storehouses or generators of these two divine principles or swiftflowing streams of blood and fire and force, the Athanor being the source or vehicle of the Serpent, and the Gluten being housed in the Cucurbite.

The manufacture of the alchemical gold which is the Dew of Immortality consists of a peculiar operation having several phases. Through the stimulus of warmth and spiritual fire to the Athanor there should be a transfer, an ascent of the Serpent from that instrument into the Cucurbite, used as a

---

[1] *Amphitheatrum*. H. Khunrath

retort[2]. The alchemical marriage or the mingling of the two streams of force in the retort causes at once the chemical corruption of the Serpent in the menstruum of the Gluten, this being the *solvé* part of the general alchemical formula of *solvé et coagula*. Hard upon the corruption of the Serpent and his death, arises the resplendent Phoenix which, as a talisman, should be charged by means of a continuous invocation of the spiritual principle conforming to the work in hand. The conclusion of the Mass consists in either the consumption of the transubstantiated elements, which is the Amrita, or the anointing and consecration of a special talisman.

By some authorities, it is roughly estimated that from the preliminary Invocation, with the binding of the force in the elements, to the act of partaking the Communion itself from the consecrated Chalice, the operation should not take less than an hour. Sometimes, indeed, a much longer period is required, especially if it is required that the charging of the talisman be complete and thorough. Great care is required to prevent the unguarded loss of the elements. There is the possibility of actual leakage or an overflowing from the Cucurbite, and the assimilation or evaporation of the corrupted elements within that instrument is also an accident greatly to be deplored. It cannot be stressed too strongly or too frequently that if the elements are not consecrated aright; or in the first place if the invoked force does not properly impinge upon or is insecurely bound within the elements, the whole operation may be nullified. And it may easily degenerate to the lowest depths, resulting in the creation of a Qliphotic horror to exist like a vampire upon the unnaturally sensitive and those who are inclined to hysteria and obsession. If the elixir be properly distilled, serving as the

---

[2] It is necessary to urge what all alchemical authorities frequently express. The application of heat should be slow and constant. Sudden rushes of heat will cause a premature ascent of the serpent into the athanor and ruin the operation.

medium of the invoked spirit, then the Heavens are opened, and the Gates swing back for the Theurgist, and the treasures of the earth are laid at his feet. "If you discover it be silent and keep it sacred. Trust to nobody but to God."

The problem of the link to connect the magical operation with the desired result should be considered in all its numerous aspects. If the Operation is one actually requiring an exterior talisman for the visible production of its effect, a suitable seal should be constructed in metal, wax, or on parchment. It may be consecrated and anointed with the elixir which has been created through the channels of the Hermetic Work. Those seals and talismans described in the *Key of Solomon the King* and *The Magus* are for the purpose quite suitable. Should it be that the operation proposed by the Theurgist is one pertaining to the qualities of Jupiter, a suitable pantacle should be prepared before the Operation. During the manufacture of the Elixir, the God-Mask of Maat should be assumed, and a conjuration of the required angel or intelligence under the governance of that God recited. Upon the completion of the Mass a minute quantity of the supernal dew should be placed on the sigil or talisman of Jupiter thus charging it with an insuperable force for the production of the desired results. Variations of this procedure will probably occur with practice.

No question of a link enters into a ceremony conducted for an end wherein the Circle and the Triangle, so to speak, or the demon and the exorcist, occupy the same plane. That is, when the Theurgist works solely upon his own consciousness without reference to any exterior effect. The Mass of the Holy Ghost, in such a case, is automatically climaxed by the consumption of the charged elements, the invoked force incarnating within the Magician as a matter of course. It is in this type of operation, I think, that the Mass of the Holy Ghost generates the greatest amount of force and ascends to the highest level of efficiency.

In the instance of operations, however, where the result desired exists on another plane or exterior to the consciousness of the Magician, effects do not always seem to follow with the same infallibility and sequence as they do in subjective workings. The perusal of private records kept by Magicians who have utilized this magical engine tend to show that it is best employed for works within the consciousness of the Magician. It is in these matters that the Mass of the Holy Ghost is the most puissant and efficacious. For the development of the Magical Will, the enhancement of the Imagination, and the Invocation both of Adonai and the Universal Gods to indwell the consecrated temple of the Holy Ghost, a better or more suitable method could hardly be devised. No expenditure of vital energy is involved, for any energy so utilized in the operation returns at the end to the Magician enhanced and enriched with the birth of the golden Phoenix, the symbol of resurrection and rebirth.

Even for ordinary operations, the great advantage of this method is that full ceremonial may be dispensed with almost altogether. The Magician quite easily can perform the banishing ritual on the Astral, and the invocations may be silently recited so that no Magic of a ceremonial nature may be perceived by the profane.

The supreme power operating in this technique is love. Trite though it may seem, and hackneyed though the word itself has become, it must be reiterated that love is the motivating power; a love force held always in leash by the Will and controlled by the Soul. The destructive power of the Sword and all that the Sword implies, the dispersive character of the dagger or the solidity or emotional inertia of the Disc or any of the other elemental weapons, has no place herein. This method therefore commends itself as being of the very highest. Since it does partake of love, it is of the stuff and essence of life itself.

In Operation, this Mass is extraordinarily simple. Indeed, one Magus has observed that it is no more complicated than the riding of a bicycle; that is to say, when once certain preliminaries and training have been encompassed. More than anything else it requires a peculiarly potent and detached

Will, arguing of course previous discipline of great severity and a mind which has been trained to Concentration for long periods of time. One of the peculiarities of this technique is that unless one is exceptionally wary and alert from the beginning it is an easy matter for the Magician to lose control of his alchemical instruments, and thus spoil the entire operation. Joy in the mere technical performance of the Mass to the exclusion of proper magical work constitutes the great and supreme danger. On the other hand, because this element of delight and joy does enter into it, this technique commands excellence over all others. The mind must be trained to concentrate under all circumstances. As a preliminary to magical practice of this kind, the technique of Yoga is a tremendous advantage. One may even state for that true success in all Magic a thorough grounding in Yoga technique is an absolute essential. And apart from skill in concentration, the practitioner should have had much experience in all kinds of magical work. He should be adept in the ceremonial charging of talismans, and have frequently preformed ceremonies for the assumption of a God form pushed to the point almost of an actual physical transformation. All the ordinary types of evocation to visible manifestation should have been mastered, and a peculiarly penetrant type of clairvoyance or spiritual vision developed. Only the magus who has had this training dare embark upon the practice of this Mass.

The general consensus of opinion of the alchemical authorities, by whom this method was esteemed, was that lofty as it was its results could not be encompassed without prayer. Without sincere prayer nothing permanent or divine could be accomplished. Hence while the Operation of the Mass is in progress, and the fire in the Athanor becomes more intense, an enthusiastic invocation, either astral or audible, should be recited. It should be in the nature of a short mantram appropriate to the nature and type of working, rhythmical in composition. The operation as a whole could be preceded by a more general invocation to legitimize the work. As the astral work of creation proceeds, the rhythmical mantram will help to formulate and vivify the moulds caused by Will and Imagination, attracting the spiritual force desired. Then, when the Serpent is transferred from the Athanor and the alchemical corruption commences in the Gluten of the White Eagle, the Cucurbite will be the receptacle of a new substance, living and dynamic, bearing the indelible impress of the invocations that will have endowed its plasticity and potentiality with an overwhelming impetus in a given direction. It will follow that with the partaking of this substance which is the philosophical Mercury, impregnated with an intelligence of dynamic spiritual energy capable of producing within the confines of its sphere the desired change, complete and satisfactory fulfillment climaxes the aspiration of the Magician.

A further observation may not be out of place. On the surface and at first sight it may appear that between this type of magical operation, so hesitatingly described, and the usual ceremonial working there exists a wide gap. It is true that the Mass of the Holy Ghost is an advance on the cumbrous and slow working of ceremonial, even although the latter is an essential at the commencement of magical training. This method is considerably more direct and to the point, and because of the peculiar class of energies which it brings to bear upon Nature, its effects are exceedingly more powerful and far-reaching than those of ceremonial alone. Nevertheless, although subsisting as two distinct classes of work, they can with great advantage be combined and used one in conjunction with the other.

Conducted within a properly consecrated Circle, after a thorough banishing, followed by a mighty conjuration of the divine force, and the assumption of the appropriate God-form, the ceremony may prove of incomparable power to open wide the Gates of the Heavens. Using solely the Cup and the Wand as elemental weapons, together with the mantram or the specialized rhythmic invocation, the Mass can seldom fail of effect. This union of two different types of magical procedure and technique, far apart though they may have appeared in the first instance, enhance the potency of each, since they combine in a single operation the finest aspects and the greatest advantages of both.

CHAPTER TWENTY SEVEN

OCCULT EUGENICS

Dr. Regardie's article presented below provides the reader with an example of the type of thinking which some occultists have attempted in recent history. You will note that the desire is to control and create a child that fits a certain set of values. I believe the article provides the exact type of evidence necessary to convince any reader who has doubts about the fundamental relationship between Magick and Science.

Occult Eugenics
by

Israel Regardie
Circa 1939

An automobile manufacturer has already familiarized us with the slogan that 'When better cars are built, Whoozis will build them.'

With apologies to this manufacturer, may I suggest a variation? 'When better babies are born, Occultism will produce them!'

Does this shock you? Does it seem flippant to you? I suppose it does, though I have not intended to be shocking or flippant. But why should this shock you? We are long accustomed to the idea that occultism is not only a philosophy of life and the universe, but what is more important a technique of living and of attainment. Occultism has familiarized us with psychological practices of different kinds, all tending towards the eventual open manifestation of the spiritual faculties of the inner man. Nor is this all.

Taboo: The Ecstasy Of Evil

Occultism has also presented us with such concepts as Reincarnation, various grades or types of souls who incarnate on this globe of ours, and the idea of karma determining amongst innumerable other things in what family and in what environment the incoming soul shall live.

What is the purpose of eugenics? Since Mendel's experiments with plants the eugenists believe that by careful breeding we ought to be able to produce a better human stock. A most laudable proposition indeed. They hold that by careful selection of parental types, a higher grade of human intelligence, efficiency and physical health should be possible. Experiments have been conducted extensively with animals. Already it is commonplace that a given breed of cattle, for example, may be considerably improved so far as those qualities which their breeders consider important. This being so, it is held that human beings are no exception to this fundamental law of development and growth.

What does occultism have to say on this score? First of all, we find that there is a good deal of objection to the basic scientific postulates. Most important amongst these objections is the widely held belief that human beings in spite of a long anterior line of physical or animal evolution, are not animals. Not being animal but mental or spiritual entities, they are not wholly subject to the physical eugenic laws already observed. This may or may not be so. Who are we to decide? A very great deal more research on chromosomes and genes, especially the mysterious X and Y chromosomes, is necessary before any final opinion can be concluded. Meanwhile, this writer does not believe that scientific explanations by themselves conduce to deep understanding. Always in biology and histology, we are confronted by fundamental questions which are not answerable without at least a mild infiltration of basic occult philosophy. Why the embryo, for example develops as it does is really a very deep mystery. Who can say why at certain set periods limb-buds and sense areas make their appearance? The observed cycle of cell multiplication from the union of sperm and ovum through the morula stage to that of the blastodermic vesicle, requires a very great deal of explaining. Why do cells divide anyway? How do they come to form a human being? What, to ask a more fundamental question, makes the centrosome split into two? More problems arise as we look deeper. These, however, are beyond my province.

But to return to an earlier philosophic point raised above, we well might argue as follows. If human beings are spiritual beings, and thereby not exclusively subject to purely mechanical laws of heredity, is there a spiritual technique of eugenics as there is a physical technique observed by cattle breeders? To my knowledge this question has not hitherto been raised. What do you think?

Well, there are many points of view. Most prominent is the theosophical one, which is that of most mystico-occult groups. Its argument would run that if two people, prospective parents, lead a pure and holy life according to the lofty ethical teachings and moral schemes laid down by Madame H.P. Blavatsky, and before her by the great spiritual teachers of mankind, then very noble and highly developed souls should be attracted to their sphere when eventually they do decide to have children. Here the emphasis is laid on morals and ethics on the type of life led, rather than on any series of exercises or meditations and practices to be performed. The facts in the case are very helpful. Children of sincere Theosophists and other occult students, as a rule, are not particularly advanced so far as concerns the especial ideals of occultism. Very often they are far less mystically inclined than their parents, to make but little mention of having far less practical ability and capacity than the child issuing from non-mystical families. Of course, the Theosophical explanation in such a case would be the introduction of the Law of Karma. The parents and the child have known each other in past incarnations, and that there are many ties—emotional, mental and physical—which have to be "worked out," to use the cliche so often employed. Old

Taboo: The Ecstasy Of Evil

debts on both sides of the ledger have to be paid. And since, often, the parents have no direct conscious knowledge of the karmic stream behind them, and which motivates them, they are therefore at the mercy of life itself or of karma (or the Unconscious) when finally they decide to have children.

This I believe to be the general occult view. It is held not only by Theosophists but by Anthroposophists and other similar groups. However, this philosophy is not especially helpful in enabling men and women deliberately to produce a higher kind of offspring. Nor does it help us in determining the sex of the unborn child—this factor of choice being a very important one.

Prior to embarking upon my thesis, mention ought to be made of Astrology. In this system there is, at least incipiently, a eugenic scheme, in spite of the fact that different astrologers interpret the facts differently. Astrologers will say that certain zodiacal or planetary types would mate well together, whilst other types in marriage would cause each other nothing but pain and unhappiness throughout. As I have said, however, the theory has never been too explicitly developed, certainly not in terms of the kind of children that might be born from such astrological marriage.

In order to ascertain whether new light can be shed upon this factor, I propose to posit as significant a technique which, unfortunately, is only too often sneered at and rejected by the ordinary run of occult students. It is to hypnotism that I refer. I do so deliberately, in spite of the fact that I know that the practice of hypnotism will immediately evoke from certain short-sighted theosophical critics such denunciations as "black magic." These I propose to ignore, reminding them that most assuredly H.P.B. did not condemn hypnotism outright nor its antecedent mesmerism, but she did object to the abuse and malpractice of unscrupulous hypnotists in their misguided experimental work. Some of the experiments performed were, I agree, absolutely damnable and no justification for them is possible. But Blavatsky herself has written "Under what circumstances is hypnotism 'black magic?' Sufficient to say that whenever the motive which actuates the operator is selfish or detrimental to any living being or beings all such acts are "black magic." Her view was that any suggestion given to a subject having a wrong or evil moral bias is to be abhorred. Suggestions having as their object the determination of whether or not a hypnotized patient would commit crime are to be shunned, her argument being that counter-suggestions may not eradicate the former suggestion from the subject's mind. In which case a positive criminal suggestion has been given which may lie dormant for years, for lives even, but being within the mind as an unconscious entity, it may at some future time or other seek expression.

Since motive, when all is said and done, is assumed to be the determining factor in this matter no real objection can be found to peopling our earth with finer and more highly developed individuals. In fact, William Quan Judge in his *Ocean of Theosophy* points out in connection with the idea of Reincarnation that there are in Devachan some remarkably highly evolved individuals—individuals who, unfortunately, have just fallen short of Mahatmaship. The devachanic period between incarnations of these Gnanis, as he calls them is exceedingly lengthy. It is our duty, he states, to provide the right kind of parents and a suitable environment whereby magnetic links can be created which will have the effect of drawing the Gnanis away from their fantastic life in Devachan into a new physical body here on earth. If our motives, then, are to attract such spiritual beings in order to better the earth with the presence of high knowledge, noble wisdom and holy people, surely any blind charge of "black magic" is undeserving of serious attention.

Before proceeding into the heart of my theorem, let me briefly state how it may be possible, for example, to determine in advance the sex of a child. We know from hypnotic experiments that suggestions during hypnotic sleep will produce a very powerful effect both on the mind and body of the patient. Suggestions can be made which will stimulate enormously the imagination of the mother. And imagination is the king faculty of our minds, a magical creative power which is "a potent help in every event of our lives," to quote H.P.B. Assuming, hence, that a young couple had decided that they wished to bless the beauty of their home with a baby, why should it not be an advantage previously to have hypnotized the mother-to-be? Suggestions could be given to her that, when she does conceive, the development of the cells within her womb from the simple cell, through all stages of embryonic life, will produce a male or female child, as their wish may be.

Fantastic? Possibly. Yet, is it any more fantastic than the host of other hypnotic feats that we know definitely to be true and veridical, and about the existence of which we have become complacent? If some argue that the sex of a child is a mechanical affair, determined by the mere accident of which spermatozoon fertilizes a certain ovum, even this argument does not invalidate the hypnotic thesis. We know that mind and the suggestions that mind makes to another mind can produce a powerful effect on the body, and upon the specific parts areas and organs of the body. It is possible to make a suggestion which would affect the sex glands and play an important role in both spermatogenesis and cogenesis. It should be possible therefore, by suggestion, to cause only a spermatozoon bearing X or Y chromosomes, to rise against the ciliary current of the female generative tract to impregnate the appropriate ovum, thus producing an embryo of the particular sex desired. Let me indicate a few of the hypnotic feats already well verified, to show that such an enterprise as I have delineated may not be wholly outside the bounds of possibility.

Delbouef, a Liege psychologist, has recorded innumerable cases of the hypnotization of a servant girl who was not too intelligent. By means of post hypnotic suggestions, she had calculated unconsciously such arithmetical examples as

11,525 seconds. Under hypnosis, it was suggested to her by Delbouef that 11,525 seconds after she awoke she would make a cross on paper and record the time. She would wake out of the hypnotic sleep completely unaware of the suggestion made, so deeply entranced was she. Some time later she would feel impelled to write. Her Unconscious had calculated the period exactly and made her record it. Moreover, surgical operations have been performed under hypnosis entirely without the use of any anaesthetic. The individual experienced no pain, during the removal, for example, of a monstrous scrotal tumor weighing over a hundred weight.

Quite recently, there was recorded in the press a case of painless delivery in childbirth. The mother of five children had been hypnotized some weeks prior to the expected event by her husband who was a psychotherapist. Suggestions had been given that no pain would be experienced. Came the time, labour began, and she was re-hypnotized. The baby was delivered, a healthy girl of eight pounds. During the birth the mother experienced no inconvenience at all, recovering much more quickly than otherwise she would have done.

By suggestion, it is possible to raise on the skin a blister within a few seconds—even as it is possible to remove a blister, likewise by suggestion. Tachycardia likewise may be overcome by hardly more than several minutes in the hypnoidal state, whereas low blood pressure and the bodily states which give rise to it will also respond quite rapidly to simple suggestions during hypnosis.

There are thousands of similar cases of cures and other phenomena that are striking and startling but these need not now be mentioned. The interested reader may refer to standard texts and casebooks for these instances. I have simply mentioned these few cases to show what is involved in the discussion. If you reflect upon the mechanism of such bodily changes as have been mentioned above, a great deal of information and insight will have been vouchsafed to you.

The smallest physical change produced through the mind by suggestion or by imagination is not less or more miraculous than some vast or unusual bodily change. In any event I am firmly convinced that the determination of sex through the same controlled employment of hypnotism is a logical development of the technique. I should like to see interested parents experiment with it under skilled guidance. At least it should prove more satisfactory and conclusive than the use of bicarbonate of soda, which until recently was employed by some medical men to influence the development of the male sex. One English psychologist to whom I spoke about this some years ago, responded very wittily by saying "Far better an alkaline boy than an acid daughter!"

The really significant question however is this—can we, quite apart from sex, improve the quality of the child? That is to say, can we beforehand arrange that, just as a cow will have certain qualities that render it invaluable to breeders, the child will possess certain mental traits, emotional characteristics and abilities that will make it an asset to the human race? Personally, I believe we can. From a prolonged study of hypnotic phenomena, I am of the opinion that suggestions made at various times during gestation will ensure that only the highest moral qualities will develop in the growing child. Not only so, but if there were prepared on the basis of sound psychology an inventory of the qualities, intellectual and emotional, such a child should have, those qualities could be induced from the conception of the foetus, and manifest themselves in the child as the years went by. Faults and failings could, because of lack of expression and development, be entirely eradicated. Think of what a generation of children we could raise! Contemplate the nature of mankind and of the earth if such a policy were definitely and officially inaugurated!

This is but one side of the practical politics. We can go much further by making use of fundamental concepts of Astrology and of certain magical techniques. In a former book of mine *The Art of True Healing* I delineated a simple but very effective technique, based upon some magical practices which were taught to the initiates of the Hermetic Order of the Golden Dawn. In making use of what is known as the Qabalistic Tree of Life, this booklet proposed the concerted employment of colour visualizations and the vibration of names and sounds in order to produce certain psychic effects within both body and mind. Magickal technique as practised within that Order and as described in my books *The Tree of Life* Now and *The Complete Golden Dawn System of Magic,* Falcon Press, 1990) could also be suitably employed with a considerable degree of success.

I am certain that a race of geniuses could be developed— geniuses of many different kinds, artistic, scientific and religious. Suppose some parents wished to have a child who was a scientist—a scientist who would assist mankind in its forward march because of his vast scientific knowledge and skill. Astrologically, we could assume that as a subject science would be included within the significance of the planet Mercury. The specific type or field of the scientist would be determined by the relation or aspect of some other planet to Mercury. For the sake of argument, let us assume it to be Jupiter. Now before conception, let us assume that husband and wife regularly and together practised a series of meditations with the object of filling themselves with the power or vibration of both Mercury and Jupiter. From traditional correspondences we know Orange to be the appropriate colour for Mercury, and the divine Name to be vibrated would be Elohim Tzavoos. Jupiter's colour would be Blue, and its sound value for vibration would be El. The technique I have elsewhere envisaged would be to visualize around these individuals on different occasions a sphere of these colours. On one occasion Orange, on another Blue. Whilst visualizing the sphere, the name is to be constantly vibrated until eventually both felt that these forces are pouring through them, permeating their minds and bodies. Hypnotism could also be included within the curriculum to ensure that a sufficiently deep impression had been made upon both parents. These techniques should be continued even after conception to ensure that the vibrations impinge without any possibility of doubt upon the embryo. The results should be that the embryo becomes so permeated by the Mercurial and Jupiterian forces, that after birth its development is psychologically and mechanically conditioned, as it were in a pre-arranged direction. Education, likewise, could be arranged accordingly, to ensure the inevitable development of the capabilities and characteristics already inherent within the child by virtue of these meditations.

Should the parents have aspirations to nurturing a future poet or artist, Venus would be the planetary force to deal with. In this event, as in the case described above, a slight knowledge of ceremonial magic would be no inconsiderable asset. That is to say, if the parents knew how to invoke the required planetary force by means of the appropriate invoking Ritual of the Hexagram and Pentagram, a much closer degree of contact with the desired force could be achieved. These techniques may sound obscure and difficult, I know. In reality they are as simple as they are effectual. The Pentagram Ritual is delineated in my work. (Note: This is included in this book.), whilst the Hexagram Ritual will be found in *The Complete Golden Dawn System of Magic.*

To conclude, may I say that this is only the briefest sketch of the possible application of the hypnotic technique. If parents will apply themselves for the sake both of their own children and of humanity, I am profoundly convinced that the results should prove eminently satisfactory. It should be possible to attract from out of Devachan or higher spiritual spheres, high and noble souls whose nature or intrinsic rhythm is of a certain planetary pattern. By embodying their psychological patterns firmly within our own minds via the imagination or by the methods described above, it is conceivable that we should draw them to us, for like attracts itself to like even as love attracts love and hatred inevitably draws hatred. High ideals and motives should likewise attract as though by a magnet similar high ideals and motives, and if our mechanism of operation is adequate, the results also should be commensurate thereto. The difficulty heretofore has been that our methods and techniques have been totally inadequate to our ideals. No doubt the method requires elucidation and more precise application. Experience will provide those details."

CHAPTER TWENTY EIGHT
THE ROYAL MASS OF THE SECRET LOVER

The following ceremony is an example of a Sexual Eucharistic Rite based on classic formulae of Western Hermeticism, (from *The Way Of The Secret Lover*, New Falcon, 1991). We have included it in it's entirety even though it makes references to talismantic images obtained in an earlier ceremony referred to as the Ultimate Divination. Unfamiliarity of the process of the Ultimate Divination should not detract from the basic understanding of the ceremony.

> (Note: This operation is Also Known As The Royal Mass of the Vault. This is used by Most High and Secret Initiates prior to Temple Initiation in the Grade of Adeptus Minor. It is done in private, prior to the Most Sacred Temple Operations. The alchemical process here will be immediately recognized by those students of the Vault of the Adepti.)

Thoth says unto him: *"Who is He whose Pylons are of Flame, whose walls of Living Uraei, and the flames of whose House are streams of Water?"*
And the Initiate replies: *"Osiris!"*
And it is immediately proclaimed: *"Thy meat shall be of the Infinite, and thy drink from the Infinite. Thou art able to go forth to the sepulchral feast on earth, for thou hast overcome."*

INITIATION AND THE SECRET LOVER

Three days prior to this operation the couple or individual must have performed the Ultimate Divination. No intercourse or sexual play should be engaged in between completing the Ultimate Divination and the Operation of the Secret Lover.

A full day should be set aside for this operation. The Sanctuary of the Royal Gnosis should be prepared the first thing in the Morning. It is advisable to have everything as new and clean as possible prior to performing this ceremony.

A day should be chosen which best represents the qualities and aspirations of the individual or couple. This can be done by simply looking at an ephemeris or by meditation.

For this operation the couple or individual shall have performed the Banishing Ritual of the Pentagram and the Middle Pillar in the Sanctuary. Remember do not concern yourselves with the results of this operation. Now is not the time.

THE OATH

I (We) Dedicate this work to my (Our) Secret Lover who is my (Our) Holy Guardian Angel.

The experience of direct divine knowledge and conversation of the Secret Lover can happen at anytime during or after the performance of these operations.

This work may be performed individually or by a couple. We will discuss this most Royal Union as if it were performed by a heterosexual couple. Let this form of discussion give no impression other than the authors are most familiar with this form of operation.

While the direct knowledge and conversation can and will be obtained by a single individual there are very specific advantages which can only be obtained by a couple. The reason for this is simple. Each partner has a Secret Lover. Thus, the four letters of Tetragrammaton are duly represented; we have the Father, Mother, Son and Daughter. The act of two has created the entire dynamic principle of the universe. Historically this aspect of the operation has been one of the best guarded secrets of the Adepts.

THE MARITAL VOW

Dearly beloved, (I or We) have come into the sight of Isis and Osiris having duly performed the necessary rituals prior to our mystical union. We have adorned and beautified our presence and this Sanctuary of the Royal Gnosis with incense, light and color. We have removed all dross from our minds and hearts and openly present ourselves, as children of light, to partake of the Eucharist which is a symbol of Divine radiance.

We charge ourselves with the secrets of the heart and sanctify this marriage with the Eucharist of our True Will.

I——— a child of light take this opportunity to cast aside the garments of darkness and take on the garments of light.

I——— a child of light take this opportunity to cast aside the garments of darkness and take on the garments of light.

Both individuals should sign this document which represents their intent and freedom in taking this action.
Each person should then repeat out loud the following:

In the presence of the Lords of the Universe I affix my signature as a sign that it is my True Will to undertake this most holy operation of the Secret Lover.
The couple should embrace and then give the sign of Shu.

Both should now say this:

Bless us, O Holy Lords, with the holy sacrament of direct and divine knowledge and conversation of our Secret Lover and may we dedicate this work and all that shall come of it to thy Holy Presence.

FIRST OPERATION

Now, the male shall be stimulated by the female a minimum of eleven times until his organ becomes his wand of inspiration. The male shall stimulate the female until her veil opens and the lustral waters of heaven pour forth.

When this is accomplished the female shall mount the male (if this be the most comfortable position). The goal of this first meeting is to exchange glances, touch the hearts, and share the first distillate of Holy Eucharist. Thus, this is a brief operation. The male and female shall not attempt to control themselves. They shall simply move as dramatically and dynamically as possible, with each movement, breathing deeply and loudly. With each breath the mind should imagine the power of the Universe entering the anus and exiting thru the anus. They should partake in the Eucharist of their creation, then bathe and rest.

SECOND OPERATION

An hour should pass between the first operation and the second operation.

The Tarot symbol from the position of Malkuth obtained in the Ultimate Divination should be brought into the Sanctuary of the Royal Gnosis.

This image, regardless of its nature, shall be focused upon until the eyes begin to tire. The symbol should then be placed in a secret and dark place. It shall act as a talisman which shall partake in the Holy Eucharist of this operation.

Later when the talisman has been consecrated with the Eucharist of the Royal Love it shall be placed in a darker and deeper place were it shall gestate and transmute for a period of one year, until the anniversary of this divine operation.

The date of this operation shall become as a Holy Day for the operants. Every year this day shall be celebrated as if it were a Birth.

Once the meditation is complete and the Tarot symbol first hidden, the couple shall regain the forces of Love through mutual stimulation. It does not matter how this is accomplished.

When the gates of the veil have been penetrated again by the wand of inspiration and the waters of heaven have lustrated this holy union, let the couple begin deep breathing, imagining that the forces of the Universe are entering the anus and exiting through the genitals.

Now this is very important. It is not simply air which one is imagining, it is the Light of the Stars of Creation itself, which enters the Anus and exits the genitals.

Thus, with each genital stroke the Holy Light of the Universe is entering the bodies and souls of the celebrants and the most profound magical exchange takes place.

This operation must be done very slowly. This is sometimes referred to as *slow heat*. At least 15 minutes should be spent in this act, so a comfortable position should be chosen.

Now, the couple shall begin to focus on the image of the Tarot symbol. This should be done in the place of Ajna (the third eye). With each breath imagine the light of the Universe entering the enjoined genitals penetrating the image at Ajna, soaking it with divine light. This should be continued for at least 10 minutes.

The couple then should drop all meditations and begin to wildly make love reaching orgasm as quickly as possible. Exhausted and before sleep ensues, the second distillate of the Eucharist should be shared with a drop of it placed upon the Tarot card in operation. The Tarot Card should now be hidden for the second and last time. The couple should then sleep or rest for at least two hours. Small amounts of food and alcohol may now be consumed. These should have been prepared ahead of time and if possible should have been kept in the Sanctuary.

THE THIRD AND SUPREME OPERATION

The Tarot symbol found in the place of Tiphareth during the Ultimate Divination shall be brought into the Sanctuary of the Royal Gnosis. It should be wrapped in a White cloth symbolizing the Holiness of the operation. The couple shall meditate upon until their eyes tire.

In this third and final operation the most divine astral nerve centers shall be stimulated. The location of work here is the Anahata (Heart) Chakkra, also, known as Tiphareth in the tradition of Western Magic.

Here is the center of Divine Harmony and the Home of the Secret Lover. It can be symbolized by Osiris, Helios, Eros or Mithra and is the goal of all true Magical operations. Its location on the Tree of Life is between Kether and Yesod, thus all psychospiritual centers of the Middle Pillar must be stimulated.

The location of Tiphareth is the point of Union were the forces of the microcosm and macrocosm unite. It is symbolized by the Hexagram and by a point in the center of the Hexagram.

Unlike, some magical or mystical operations which take place only in the Imagination, this final operation will take place in the Imagination but also in the body and soul of the aspirant. This union of Imagination and Body is completely in adherence with the goal of all True Western Magical Operations as demonstrated by the most ancient and powerful initiations and alchemies.

The couple should jointly perform the Banishing Rituals of the Pentagram and Hexagram.

The following prayer should be said jointly. As the couple repeats the prayer let them "enflame" themselves with the power of Love.

> I am Toom, the Setting Sun, I am the only being in the firmament of Heaven.
> I am Ra, the Rising Sun, I have passed from the Gate of Death unto Life.
> The Sun's power beginneth again after he hath set; he riseth again (so doth the justified Spirit of Man.)
> I am the Great God begotten of himself; I can never be turned back by the Elementary Powers; I am the Morning, I Know the Gate. (I ever rise again unto existence. I know the pathway through death unto life.)
> The Father of the Spirit; the Eternal Soul of the Sun. He hath examined and He hath proved me. He hath found that I fought on Earth the battle of the good Gods, as He, my Father, Lord of the Invisible World ordered me to do.
> I know the Great God who existeth in the Invisible.
> I am the Great Phoenix which is in Annu, the former of my Life and my Being am I.

In order to activate the correct image of the entire Tree of Life which includes the pillars of Severity and Mercy symbolized by the Crook and Scourge of Osiris the following should be read a day or two before the operation.

Thus, while you symbolize the Middle Pillar, you have neatly placed in your subconscious the Pillars of Severity and Mercy to be activated when and will they wish in this most Sacred Sanctuary of the Royal Gnosis.

THE IMAGE TO BE PLACED IN THE MIND

Once the "Soul" has passed through the ordeal (refers to death, judgement, etc.) it is "...then introduced into the

Taboo: The Ecstasy Of Evil

Presence of Osiris by Horus. Osiris sits in his Shrine upon a throne, with the Crook and Scourge, symbols of Mercy and Severity in his hands; behind him are Isis and Nephthys, the Goddesses of Nature and Perfection; and before him are the four Genii of the Dead upon the Lotus Flower, the emblem of the Metempsychosis. Thus the whole of the Symbols upon the pillars represent the advance and purification of the Soul, and its uniting with Osiris the Redeemer; in that Golden Dawn of an Infinite Light wherein the soul is transfigured; knows all and can do all; for it hath become joined unto Eternal Gods."

The wand of power and the veil (Gate) of the Sanctuary should be brought into operation. It is of the upmost importance that the couple be fortified for this operation as it must exhaust them. They are coupling their will and desire for direct and divine knowledge and communication with the Holy Guardian Angel, "against" the desire of the body to give in—let go—and "die" at its will. Thus, they are creating an intense spiritual heat.

Thus, this act the charging the Eucharist is created by the eternal process of birth, death and resurrection and is fully symbolized and enacted by complete Surrender.

The couple should choose a position which allows the altar (the bed) to support them.

When they have joined they should begin breathing taking first in the Light through the anus and allowing it to flow through and out of the Anahata. This should be done for 10 minutes. Remember with each slow rhythmic breath the wand and the veil should be slowly stimulated by movement.

Next they should allow the Light of the Universe to flow thru Sahasrara, the lotus of the thousand petals, the Chakkra positioned directly above the head, the home of Amoun and Ptah. The Light should flow out of Anahata, the home of the Secret Lover. This should be done for 10 minutes.

Next, the Light of the Universe should emerge from the genitals, the home of Shu, and flow thru Anahata. This should be done for 10 minutes.

Finally, the Light of the Universe should emerge *from* Anahata and flow *thru* Anahata. This should be done for 10 minutes.

(Note: The invisible Sephirah Daath has been deliberately left out in this operation; those familiar with it and its holy name may use it.)

When this is completed the couple should wildly and passionately make love surrendering themselves to the Ecstasy of the Secret Lover. Upon satisfaction, the third distillate Eucharist should be shared. The couple should be quiet being open to the presence of the All. This moment has been called by the Wise—The Epiphany.

Later, the Tarot symbol from the location of Tiphareth should be adored and anointed with the Elixir. This symbol should be also hidden and left undisturbed for one year.

The Sanctuary of the Royal Gnosis should be closed with the Banishing Ritual of the Pentagram.

This is then the act of establishing Direct and Divine Knowledge and Conversation of the Holy Guardian Angel. Practice this ritual as often as necessary to assure that a deep and everlasting contact is made. The Epiphany will lengthen and increase in intensity with practice.

The energies of Love feed the relationship and the Secret Lover will satisfy itself with the joy that it will take in you.

Your Secret Lover will be your Lover and your guide throughout your engagement on this planet, as well as your guide in the afterlife.

CHAPTER TWENTY NINE

THE MYSTICAL/MAGICKAL MEANING OF THE ROYAL MASS

The Royal Mass is the synthesis of many complicated and complex magickal operations. Some have said that within it lay the quintessence of all that Man yearns for in this life.

While the Mass is a magickal operation, its goal is purely "mystical" (if we mean by that term union with the Divine). More, the Royal Mass is both transpersonal as well as personal. Thus, the Mass meets the requirements of Magick, Mysticism and strangely enough, psychosexuality. The openness and emotional depth of the Royal Mass requires of the couple a love and freedom typically unknown in "normal" sexuality which has been overburdened by guilt, obsession and shrouded with obligations.

(1) The magickal tone of the operation is in the various rituals and the making of talismans. Unlike most talismans which have a quality of deadness about them, those made from the Royal Mass are charged with the power and joy of the Universe; thus they are alive with the force of growth and infinite possibility.

(2) The mystical tone of the Royal Mass is in the invocation of the Holy Guardian Angel who becomes the Lover of the participant. Thus, the requirement of surrender, which most mystics clamor about but rarely have an idea how to reach, is legitimately met.

Even at this point the Royal Mass meets the Supreme goal dreamed of by aspirants from the beginning of time. Individuality is absorbed into the infinite and maintained separately, fulfilling the obvious requirement that the Universe has set the stage for both Individuality and Union.

The Universe demands both Ego and Non-Ego and any attempt to pass one as the other will mean complete defeat in this operation.

The fact that the operators start and direct the process and then surrender to their own creation only to find something more shows the utmost respect for "Ego and Non-Ego." There is no either/or here, the curse of the average religionist.

(3) The psychosexual component can best be appreciated in the context of the "normal" human relationship which can best be understood by what is missing from it—everything.

As a one time psychotherapist I abandoned psychotherapy when it finally struck me that no true healing could occur within the context of legislated mental health, except that of a Doctor fixing a broken leg, which of course is very important for the man in pain. I came to the realization that the repaired leg might even be better than it was before, but still a "leg is not a wing."

Thus, when properly performed the Royal Mass transforms the psychosexual component of life making it more than ever imagined.

THE FORMULA OF YHVH

In this most sacred and powerful Magickal act the Supreme force is Love; Love under Will.

The lustral waters and the blood of life mingle in a Thunderous embrace. Each mixing and renewing the earth with life. All necessary divisions come to an end in the frenzied excitement of the moment. The YH (Yod, Heh), the Father and Mother become VH (Vau, Heh(f)), the Prince and the Princess who then become the Father and Mother again. The couple transform into the ultimate magical weapon—the Cup and the Wand united—the Cucurbite (the crystal jewelled vessel) and the Athanor (the divine furnace). The substance created from this alchemical marriage, the Celestial Dew, becomes the Eucharist of the Communion.

Within this entire process a new lover emerges—The Secret Lover (the Holy Guardian Angel.)

For the first time we see true love, equal and diverse, a cooperation for the benefit of all without an external moral commandment to assure and monitor its success. No one loses. (No doubt something must be wrong here—doesn't someone always have to lose?)

Power, Love, Self Mastery, Surrender, Ego, Non Ego, the Sun and the Moon, these are the results of the Royal Mass. Love under Will.

CHAPTER THIRTY

THE CEREMONY OF THE SUN AND MOON

In the traditions of many of the world's great religions, the consummation of marriage is considered holy. It is ironic that even in Orthodox Christianity (where sex is viewed as the Original Sin whereby all mankind incarnates) marriage is recognized as one of the Seven Sacraments or Mysteria along with baptism, chrismation, confession, ordination, holy unction and *holy Eucharist*. Indeed, if all Christians embarked upon the chaste asceticism of the Apostles and early followers of Christ, the Church might have died out in short order.

The stable influence of the institution of marriage has historically provided the Church with a harvest of advantages. She has been guaranteed a perpetual and growing membership whose potentiality for sexual "mischief," if not eliminated, is at least regulated.

Below is a "Marriage" ritual of the Thelemic Order of the Golden Dawn which granted us permission to print it in its entirety. The God-forms the participants assume are from the Thelemic pantheon. The Priestess is Nuit, the star Goddess of the Night Sky—the universe expanded—the circumference of the Cosmic Circle. In the more immediate environment of our Solar System She is the Moon. The Priest is Hadit Her lover. He too is infinite. But the infinite contraction of the universe—the point in the center of the Cosmic Circle. His Symbol in the Solar System is the Sun.

Here we have two infinites, one ultimately expanded and large, one totally contracted and small. Now, if the circumference is infinite and the center is infinite, they are both equally everywhere! They are always in contact. They touch, they rub, they embrace everywhere—lovers on a truly cosmic scale. This interplay of eternal contraction and expansion of two opposing infinites creates the finite. This finite field of operation is the foundation of the phenomenal universe and is represented in the ritual by Ra-Hoor-Khuit, the Crowned and Conquering Child, the Lord of the present Aeon, who represents the transcendent Self of each of us.

THE CEREMONY OF THE SUN AND MOON

Being a Ritual of Marriage designed for the Conjoining of two souls in Nuit and Hadit.

Official Ceremony of the Novus Ordo Aureae Aurora

By
David Cherubim

Do what thou wilt shall be the whole of the Law.

I
THE ARRANGEMENT OF THE TEMPLE

The Temple shall be arranged accordingly: In the centre shall be the Altar, having upon it a Cup of Wine, two Cakes of Light, the Magick Wand, the Magick Bell, the Holy Oil, two Magical Links for the Priest and the Priestess (two consecrated Rings), and The Book of the Law.

II
THE PREPARATION OF THE CEREMONY

The Priest shall wear a Red (or White) Robe and the Priestess shall wear a Blue (or Black) Robe to symbolize Fire and Water (or Light and Darkness, that is, Male and Female). The Priest shall wear a Lamen of the Sun and the Priestess shall wear a Lamen of the Moon. They shall duly purify their bodies before they robe.

To begin this Holy Ceremony of the Sun and Moon, let the Priest duly banish in the Temple by the proper magical method. (Perform the Banishing Ritual of the Star Ruby, Liber XXV). Then shall he apply the Holy Oil to himself and the Priestess shall do the same to herself, consecrating their Wills to this Great Work of Union. Then shall they kiss, uniting hands as they do so. Then shall they position themselves in their appropriate stations in the Temple, the Priest in the East of the Temple and the Priestess in the West of the Temple, facing each other.

Before conducting this Holy Ceremony, the Priest and the Priestess should meditate in their hearts upon verses 33 and 34 of Chapter I of *The Book of the Law*. Also they should meditate in their hearts upon verse 35 of Chapter II of *The Book of the Law*. Let them perform this Holy Ceremony in accordance with these holy injunctions of Thelema. They should especially meditate upon and put into proper effect the holy injunction: "the rituals shall be half known and half concealed:"

III
THE PROCLAMATION AND THE OATH

Priest:	(In the East facing Priestess in the West) Do what thou wilt shall be the whole of the Law.
Priestess:	(In the West facing Priest in the East) Love is the law, love under will.
Priest:	What is thy Will, O Lady of the Night?
Priestess:	It is my Will to sacramentally Unite. And what is thy Will, O Man of the Sun?
Priest:	It is my Will to become as One.
Priestess:	And by what Magick Spell shall we work our Will?
Priest:	By the Spell of this Ritual's Mystick Seal.
Priestess:	And what shall we make by this act Unknown?

Priest	A mysterious object called the Philosopher's Stone!
Priestess:	Art thou prepared to do thy Will?
Priest:	I am prepared to accomplish the Grand Miracle.
Priestess:	Will you take an Oath to complete this Rite?
Priest:	I will take the Oath and we will Unite.
Priestess:	Then seal thy words with a precious Kiss And so shall we unite in infinite Bliss!

The Priest and Priestess go to the Altar and the Priest kisses his Priestess on her lips. Then shall they unite hands above *The Book of the Law* on the Holy Altar, and together they shall take the Oath.

Priest and Priestess:
In freedom we take this Oath of love
To accomplish our Will on earth as above!
We promise and swear, and infinitely aspire,
To unite as one—our hearts desire!
By Fire and Water we will partake this hour
The Holy Sacrament of Magick Power!
And so shall we work our Will to Unite
And attain the Quintessence of the Rite!
This Oath we promise; this Oath we swear
As we enflame ourselves with Prayer!
In the Name of Thelema—the Law of Liberty,
As we will, So mote it be!

IV
THE INVOCATION OF THE ELEMENTS

The Priest advances to the appropriate Elemental quarters and invokes the Elements by way of the Unicursal Hexagram and the appropriate verbal invocations.

(Priest advances to the East, traces the Unicursal Hexagram of Earth, and invokes:)

Holy art Thou, O Lord of the Earth,
Thou Lord of Life, our essence of birth!
O thou soul of all forms that we see,
Come Thou forth we say unto Thee!

(Priest goes to the South, traces the Unicursal Hexagram of Fire, and invokes:)

Holy art Thou, O Lord of the Fire,
Thou Lord of Light, to which we aspire!
O Thou Flashing Flame of Eternity,
Come Thou forth we say unto Thee!

(Priest goest to the West, traces the Unicursal Hexagram of Water, and invokes:)

Holy art Thou, O Lord of the Water,
Thou Lord of Love and Mystick Rapture!
O Thou inscrutable Depth of the Sea,
Come Thou forth we say unto Thee!

(Priest goes to the North, traces the Unicursal Hexagram of Air, and invokes:)

Holy art Thou, O Lord of the Air,
Thou Lord of Liberty, to which we adhere!
O Thou perpetual Breath of Ecstasy,
Come Thou forth we say unto Thee!

(The Priest now goes to the Centre of the Temple, completing the Circle. He then gives the Sign of the Cross, and declares:)

Holy art thou, ye Elements Divine,
Invoked and inspired to perfectly combine
In this Temple consecrated to Love
To accomplish below That which is Above!

V
THE INVOCATION OF THE SUN AND MOON

The Priest and Priestess now exchange stations, so that the Priest is facing East and the Priestess is facing West.

Priest   (Makes Unicursal Hexagram of Sol, and invokes:)

I Invoke Thee, O Thou Glorious Sun,
To come Thou forth that our Will be done!
Let Thy Light illumine this Temple
Making true the Magick of this Holy Ritual!

Priestess   (Makes Unicursal Hexagram of Luna, and invokes:)

I invoke Thee, O Thou Soul of Night,
To come Thou forth that we may Unite!
Let Thy Love work its Mighty Spell
To make as one, both Heaven and Hell!

VI
THE CONJOINING OF THE SUN AND MOON

The Priest and Priestess shall now unite to produce the Philosopher's Stone, that they may duly charge their Magical Links with the invoked Current of this Sacramental Ceremony of Love for the accomplishment of their Will to Unite. When this is complete, let the Priest consume the Elixir and administer the same unto his Priestess.

VII
THE CHARGING OF THE MAGICAL LINKS

A portion of the Philosopher's Stone shall be used to charge the Magical Links which are designed to bring about the desired magical effect of this Holy Ceremony. They shall be imbued with the invoked force of the Stone. These links should be in the form of consecrated Magical Rings which shall be worn by the Priest and Priestess as true tokens of their consummation of this Sacramental Ceremony. The Priest shall do best by tracing the Sigil of the Moon on the Ring which he will administer to his Priestess, and the Priestess shall do best by tracing the Sigil of the Sun on the Ring which she will administer to her Priest.

Priest (When tracing Sigil of Luna, let him declare:)

This ring I bless to unite my soul
With the Priestess of this Holy Ritual!

> The Priest shall now kiss the Ring and place it on the proper finger of his Priestess.

Priestess (When tracing Sigil of Sol, let her declare:)

This ring I bless to unite my soul
With the High Priest of this Holy Temple!
> The Priestess shall now kiss the ring and place it on the proper finger of her Priest.

VIII
THE PROCLAMATION OF THE RINGS OF POWER

Both Upon our fingers there is Magick Power,
Rings of a Spell, by which we empower
Our Will to unite in Love and Liberty—
A Mystic delight for all eternity!
These Rings of Love we do proclaim
As Links of a Power we do acclaim!
By their Magick we enforce our Way
To work our Will both Night and Day!

IX
THE PROCLAMATION OF THE UNION OF THE SUN AND MOON

Both   This we proclaim: that we are Bound
In Mystick Love and Freedom Profound!
Our divided souls are wed in Ecstasy:
We are ever joined in Love and Liberty!

This we Proclaim; that we are One:
In the Sun and Moon our Will is Done!
We shall now celebrate with Wine and Cake
This blessed Union which we undertake!

X
THE CELEBRATION OF THE SUN AND MOON

Both   We partake the Cake; we partake the Wine:
The bread and the blood—sacraments divine!

Let the Priest and the Priestess now partake the Cakes and the Wine. When this is duly accomplished, they shall then declare:

Both   We revel with joy in this act of Zeal,
Partaking the elements with Love under Will!

The Priest and Priestess shall now embrace their bodies in pure passionate ecstasy and joy, ending all with a sacramental kiss of delicious delight as a final token of their Mystick Love.

XI
THE GREAT WORK ACCOMPLISHED

The Priest and Priestess shall now strike the Magick Bell. The Priestess shall hold the Bell on High, and the Priest shall strike the Bell 3-5-3 with his Wand. When this is duly accomplished, they shall then both proclaim:

ABRAHADABRA!

This final Word of Power seals this Sacramental Ceremony of Love with the Magical Current of the Great Work of Thelema, of which it is a proper magical glyph, being the glyph of the Magick Formula of the Mystick Union of the Rose and Cross. It is the Great Reward of Our Lord Ra-Hoor-Khuit, administered unto them who are chosen and united in Nuit and Hadit.

To properly end this Holy Ceremony, the Priest shall duly perform the Banishing Ritual of the Star Ruby (Liber XXV). Then shall the Priest and Priestess depart the Temple in unison, with hands joined to symbolize their going forth together to do their Will among the legions of the living; yea, to do their Will among the legions of the living.

Love is the law, love under will.

CHAPTER THIRTY ONE

ANGELIC SEX MAGICK

Sex Magick is not limited to the Tantric or alchemical practitioners alone. The power of skillfully directed sexual energy is limited only by the abilities of the individuals directing that energy. Every human being who has experienced orgasm has momentarily unleashed that power. The subjective images and thoughts that rush through the mind in the afterglow of sex are profound visions waiting to be acknowledged.

The traditional forms of ceremonial magick, such as Goetia (the evocation of one of 72 classic spirits into a triangle) or Enochian Magick (Evocation and Invocation of the Angelic beings of the Elements and the 30 levels of the heavens) have not, by exoteric tradition, incorporated sexual applications. Esoteric teachings on these subjects, however, indicate a far different attitude.

Below are two essays which are indicative of the ease with which the fundamentals of Sex Magick can be applied to heretofore nonsexual magical disciplines. They are excerpted from our book on Enochian Evocation; *The Enochian World of Aleister Crowley—Enochian Sex Magick* (New Falcon Publications 1991). The Authors wish to remind the reader that the following is provided for illustrative purposes only. It may appear there is adequate information below to begin the practices outlined, but we strongly urge a thorough grasp of the subject before any practical applications are attempted.

DIVINE EROTICISM

Intimate union of the worshipper with the Divine Principal is a central theme of religion. It is quite natural that the

Taboo: The Ecstasy Of Evil

images which are evoked by the Devotee in his ardor for the Beloved are identical or similar to those that accompany sexual longings. The traditional cultures of India and the Orient, of Africa, Polynesia, of the natives of North and South America, indeed of almost any culture unpolluted by Judeo-Christian-Islamic thought, have no difficulty whatsoever with this parallel.

With the exception of the *Song of Solomon*, Western religious literature avoids Divine Eroticism like the plague. Even the esoteric disciplines of the West seem uncomfortable with the subject and go to great lengths to veil their terms. The bizarre nomenclature of Alchemy, when studied with half your brain in the bedroom, reveals that perhaps there are several good reasons why the alchemists were called "puffers". But for the most part, we in the West are expected to unite with our Divine Beloved vicariously.

Nuns are the "Brides of Christ", we unite with the Father or the Mother only "through the Son." Even the "magic" ceremony needed to consummate these voyeuristic unions must be experienced vicariously through a priest.

I do not intend to use this space to serve as an introduction to the theories or techniques of Sex Magick or Tantra. There are many fine works available that introduce those subjects very well. For the reader who is already knowledgeable on these subjects, a few helpful hints concerning how elements of Enochian evocation can be used in these areas may prove valuable and rewarding.

The modern view that our normal waking consciousness stands somewhere between the limitless potential of transcendental experience and the "demons" that run amok in our subconscious mind is not too dissimilar to the medieval view that Mankind is sandwiched between God and the Angels, between Heaven and Hell. The working hypothesis of the magician of old went something like this, "God has dominion over me and compels me to do His will. I have dominion over the spirit world, (especially over the so-called fallen angels), and just as I look up to God, they look up to me, therefore I can compel them to do my bidding."

In 1458, the noted Qabalist and court magician, Abraham the Jew, in his classic work, *The Book of the Sacred Magick of Abra-Melin The Mage*, took this concept of the hierarchy of responsibility a sublime step forward and catapulted magick to the same level as the Yogic disciplines.

Simply put, to work the magick, you must first be united with Divinity. (This experience he calls The Knowledge and Conversation of the Holy Guardian Angel.) This initiatory landmark is only accomplished after a six month period of purification and a strict regimen of ever-increasing longing for union with the Angel. Once this "marriage" is consummated and the "blessing" of the Angel's presence is bestowed, the magician immediately turns to the lower spiritual world and bestows the same "blessing" on the resident denizens and extracts from them a pledge of loyalty and support.

These wild and infernal spirits who, up until now were unacknowledged, uncontrolled and most likely at odds with the True Will of the magician, were now going to be given the opportunity to work for his and their greater good. And now that the magician had formed an intimate alliance with the Divine, he had the spiritual "authority" to force the lower spirits to co-operate.

Thus, Abraham the Jew reveals an indispensable truth; Magick demands an assault on two fronts at once. It requires realization of your responsibility not only to that which is above but also to that which is below.

It is only through *you* that the Divine (your Superconsciousness) can manifest on this plane. Without *you* the spirits of the Infernal regions (your subconsciousness) have no hope of "salvation" (balance and control). Indeed, without your controlling influence they will become a very real threat to your life and sanity. You must see to it that each area receives proper and equal attention. Neglect your higher aspiration and you will find that you soon lack the spiritual integrity to command the spirits. Neglect the spirits and they will sooner or later surface to demand your attention. Wild beasts can be domesticated and trained to serve you. If you treat them well and allow them to share in your continuing good fortune they can realize their greater potentiality. However, if you abuse them or forget to feed them they will inevitably seize the first opportunity to break out and devour you for their needed nourishment.

The two pillars of the Enochian system, as outlined in the classic work on Enochian evocation, *Liber Chanokh* are:

I
THE ELEMENTAL WATCH-TOWERS OF THE UNIVERSE AND THE TABLET OF UNION
(The World of the Elemental Beings)

II
THE THIRTY ÆTHYRS WHOSE DOMINION EXTENDETH IN EVER-WIDENING CIRCLES WITHOUT AND BEYOND THE WATCH-TOWERS OF THE UNIVERSE.
(The World of the Divine Beings)

Both these worlds can be explored sexually and can provide the diligent magician with the joy and fulfillment of his or her Divine Beloved and the passion and energy of being the Divine Beloved to an Elemental lover.

Please pay special attention to the following.

ENOCHIAN SEX MAGICK

But to love me is better than all things

Liber AL, I, 61

In the series of visions of the 30 Æthyrs that Aleister Crowley chronicled in his remarkable work, *The Vision And The Voice*, he describes his vision of the Body of the great Goddess. The imagery is so powerful and his narrative colored with expressions of such tender awe, that one cannot but share, however temporarily, his overwhelming desire to unite with Her. To lose oneself utterly in Her would most certainly result in such intensity of bliss as to make the ecstasy of orgasm seem as a candle held up to the sun.

But that was Crowley's vision...Crowley's Great Goddess. To dwell on Her when you have your own Great Goddess (or God) "waiting" for your devotion would be as stupid as refusing a date with the lovely girl next door (who has secretly loved you all her life) because you have to sit at home alone, and pine over a painting of Helen of Troy.

Do you see where I'm heading with this? By a serious and concerted effort on your part, it is possible for you to achieve the highest level of spiritual experience your evolutionary-initiatory status will permit, including a relationship with the Divine Beloved. Once you "know" Her (or Him) all subsequent "earthly" ecstasies take the form of devotional offerings to the Great Lover who rewards the devotee with increasingly sweeter embraces until finally the embrace is eternal.

Where do you seek the initial Vision?

In yourself.

How can you start to look in yourself?

One way is by systematically skrying the 30 Æthyrs of the Enochian system.

> *Nor let the fools mistake love; for there are love and love. There is the dove, and there is the serpent.*
> *Choose ye well!*
>
> Liber AL, I, 57

In *The Little Mermaid*, Hans Christian Andersen writes of an Undine who is so enamored of a mortal man that she relinquishes her status as an immortal being for the opportunity to love and be loved by him. This charming tale contains a profound magical truth. Elemental spirits, whose natures are so specialized that they lack the balance of qualities necessary for sentient life, do indeed long for union with "complete" beings such as ourselves. Because their natures are universal they truly are immortal and if they should ever achieve union with a mortal they would actually "die" to their old, incomplete existence to be "born" into the life of their beloved. This is exactly what *we* do in our relationship with the Divine Principal.

The spirits of the Enochian Elemental Tablets are particularly suitable for such operations and all that is required is to call them up. It is so simple that you may set to work ill-prepared for success. A few words of caution might be in order.

Think before you proceed. Just what are you really prepared to handle? Experience has shown that it is most often wisest to contact a spirit from very low in the elemental hierarchy for operations such as this. Also, as in the everyday world, it is unwise to try to juggle too many of these relationships at the same time. If you think "Hell hath no fury like that of a *woman* scorned," think again. And sometimes jealousy *really is* a *green-eyed monster*.

Finally, and most importantly, *Never confuse your love for the Divine with your love for the Elemental*. The sexual "role" the magician assumes when making love to the Goddess (or God) is diametrically different than the "role" he or she plays when mating with an elemental spirit. In the former, the magician's attitude is that of adoration and awe and release is a gift from above, the result of ecstatic surrender. (To assume that attitude with an elemental lover would be spiritual suicide.) The sexual "role" the magician assumes with the elemental is one of loving dominance. The Spirit surrenders to you. You bestow your ecstasy as a gift and allow your elemental partner to share, through you, the Divine love.

Confusing these two "loves" is surely the fountainhead of all the ills sexual repression has visited upon mankind. If it is your Will to be a Sex Magician, see to it that you use your magick to face and conquer your life, not to hide from it.

CHAPTER THIRTY TWO

TECHNIQUES OF ENOCHIAN SEX MAGICK

There is no evidence that the communicating Angels that delivered the Enochian system to Dr. John Dee and Edward Kelly ever instructed them concerning sexual applications of the art.

Biographers will be quick to point out the famous incident of April 1587 when, according to Kelly, the Angel Madimi suggested to Kelly that he and Dr. Dee share their wives in common. (Dee was absent during this communication.) Enochian scholars argue that the text of this communication contains many flaws that do not characterize other less *personal* communications and that this may have been a case of magical wishful thinking on Kelly's part. Nevertheless, it seems they did indeed swap wives and in spite of obvious attempts to erase the manuscript, the record confirms this. It seems the only "magical" result of this "operation" was the break up of Dee and Kelly as magical partners and the close of one of the most remarkable chapters in magical history.

To those knowledgeable in the theory and techniques of Tantra, the keys of the Enochian system open a treasure-house of practical applications.

The exercises outlined below should be practiced only after you have a thorough mastery of the system in all its non-sexual applications. Any uncertainties on the part of the magician as to what he or she is doing will destroy needed concentration and create a "break" which will absorb the entire force of the operation. (In sexual workings that could be an overabundant amount of energy particularly if you perform the exercises in my Tantra book.)

EXPLORATION OF THE THIRTY ÆTHYRS

As written earlier in the text, the Thirty Æthyrs are the "heavens" or Aires of the system. Starting with the 30th Æthyr and working to the 1st, the Magician explores only as far as his or her personal level of Initiation will permit. This process is comparable to "pathworkings" of the Qabalistic system. In Enochian terms, the "Great Work" of the magician is to master all 30 Æthyrs. (Starting with 30 and ending with 1) Experiences with the 30 Æthyrs are highly personal and entirely unique to each magician. Working with the Æthyrs can be a lifetime endeavor and it is entirely presumptuous and inappropriate for another individual to "guide" another in this area.

This personal aspect of the Æthyrs coupled with the simplicity of its "one-Call-does-it-all" procedure makes it ideal for preliminary workings.

The great stumbling block to exploring the Æthyrs is the difficulty one encounters in "breaking through" to the next Æthyr. In the higher levels this may be because the magician has reached his or her initiatory limit. But in the lower Æthyrs it is more often the case that the magician simply can't "let go" and refocus his or her attention to the section of the brain where the vision is taking place. In *Secrets of Western Tantra* I provide an entire array of exercises which will help the Magician "let go."

The following exercise is intended exclusively for workings of the Thirty Æthyrs. There are two participants whom we will refer to as the Magician and the Assistant. For our illustration the male participant is the Magician and will recite the Call and "receive" the vision, the female participant is the Assistant and will eventually record the vision. These gender roles are for illustration only. The Magician can just as easily be female and the Assistant male. This particular operation is equally effective for participants of the same sex and can also be adapted for solitary workings. *It makes absolutely no difference who is Magician and who is*

Assistant. It is only important that the couple decide before the operation commences.

Note: There must be no ambiguity about the willingness of either participant to take part in an operation of this kind. If one participant has to be coerced, begged or tricked into participation the vortex of ill-will that will emanate from the offended party will insure not only the failure of the operation but also the destruction of a more precious "magical asset", the respect of another human being.

The Magician wishes to explore the 30th Æthyr, **TEX**, and the Assistant has expressed to him that it is her Will to participate in the operation.

Both participants bathe and dress at first in simple, soft, white garments. You may light incense, burn candles or use lights or soft music to enhance the mood. Small amounts of alcohol are also useful.

EXAMPLE

Prepare the room in which you are working with the appropriate symbols for the Æthyr such as the sigils of the Governors or the Elemental Tablet from which they are taken. In the case of **TEX** it would be the Water Tablet. (One couple I know has the Elemental Tablets and the Tablet of Union constructed entirely of wooden pyramids which they painstakingly have painted and lettered in Enochian. These are placed on the floor, under their bed, prior to æthyric or elemental workings.)

Begin by performing the Lesser Banishing Ritual of the Pentagram in the area in which you will be working.

THE LESSER BANISHING RITUAL OF THE PENTAGRAM

The Qabalistic Cross
facing east:

    Touch your forehead and say **Atoh (aah—toh)**
    Touch your Heart and say **Malkuth (mal—kooth)**
    Touch your Right Shoulder and say **Ve—Geburah (veh—gheb—oo—rah)**
    Touch your Left Shoulder and say **Ve—Gedulah (veh—ghed—oo—lah)**
    Touch your Heart and say **Le—Olam (luh—oh—lahm)**
    Point the symbolic dagger inward and say **Amen (aah—mayn)**.

Still facing East:

Trace the Banishing pentagram of Earth and vibrate **YHVH (yoad—hay—vaahv—hay)**, as you thrust your symbolic dagger into the heart of the pentagram.

    With your arm still extended,
    turn to the South:

Trace the Banishing pentagram of Earth and vibrate the name **ADONAI (aah—doh—noy)**. {Remember to thrust the symbolic dagger as you vibrate each God name}.

    With your arm still extended,
    turn to the West:

Trace the Banishing pentagram of Earth and vibrate the name **EHIEH (eh—hayh—yay)**.
    With your arm still extended,
    turn to the North:
Trace the Banishing pentagram of Earth and vibrate the name **AGLA (ah—guh—lah)**.

With your arm still extended return to the East, completing the circle. Now Imagine yourself surrounded in a Flaming Circle of four Pentagrams.

Stand straight with your arms out forming the shape of a Cross:

Say:

>Before me **Raphael (rah—fay—ale)**
>Behind me **Gabriel (gah—bree—ale)**
>At my right shoulder, **Michael (mee—khigh—ale)**
>At my left shoulder, **Auriel (oh—ree—ale)**

Then Say:

>Before me **flames the Pentagram**
>Behind me shines the **six-rayed Star**.
>
>Finish by repeating the Qabalistic Cross:
>
>Touch your forehead and say **Atoh**
>Touch your Heart and say **Malkuth**
>Touch your Right Shoulder and say **Ve—Geburah**
>Touch your Left Shoulder and say **Ve—Gedulah**
>Touch your Heart and say **Le—Olam**
>Point the symbolic dagger inward and say **Amen.**

The Magician then recites the Call of the 30th Æthyr, **TEX** while the Assistant simply relaxes and meditates upon the sounds of the Enochian Call.

Taboo: The Ecstasy Of Evil

THE CALL OF THE 30TH ÆTHYR

MADARIATZA das perifa **TEX** cahisa micaolazoda saanire caosago od fifisa balzodizodarasa Iaida. Nonuca gohulime: Micama adoianu MADA faoda beliorebe, soba ooaona cahisa luciftias peripesol, das aberaasasa nonucafe netaaibe caosaji od tilabe adapehaheta damepelozoda, tooata nonucafe jimicalazodoma larasada tofejilo marebe yareryo IDOIGO od torezodulape yaodafe gohola, Caosaga, tabaoreda saanire, od caharisateosa yorepoila tiobela busadire, tilabe noalanu paida oresaba, od dodaremeni zodayolana. Elazodape tilaba pare-meji peripesatza, od ta qurelesata booapisa. Lanibame oucaho sayomepe, od caharisateosa ajitoltorenu, mireca qo tiobela lela. Tonu paomebeda dizodalamo asa pianu, od caharisateosa aji-la-tore-torenu paracahe a sayomepe. Coredazodizoda dodapala od fifalazoda, lasa manada, od faregita bamesa omaoasa. Conisabera od auauotza tonuji oresa; catabela noasami tabejesa leuitahemonuji. Vanucahi ome-petilabe oresa! Bagile? Moooabe OL coredazodizoda. El capimao itzomatzipe, od cacocasabe gosaa. Bajilenu pii tianuta a babalanuda, od faoregita teloca uo uime.

Madariiatza, torezodu!!! Oadariatza orocaha aboaperi! Tabaori periazoda aretabasa! Adarepanu coresata dobitza! Yolacame periazodi arecoazodiore, od quasabe qotinuji! Ripire paaotzata sagacore! Umela od peredazodare cacareji Aoiveae coremepeta! Torezodu! Zodacare od Zodameranu, asapeta sibesi butamona das surezodasa Tia balatanu. Odo cicale Qaa, od Ozodazodama pelapeli IADANAMADA!

When the Call is completed let the Magician slowly vibrate the names of the Governors. (In the case of **TEX** there are four Governors. All other Æthyrs have three.)

Then, (believe it or not), forget about the operation. Relax, take your time and enjoy each other's company. Build slowly and naturally to greater levels of arousal. Continue to do everything you can to sustain your love making (At least 25 minutes, but for God's sake don't keep looking at your watch!). The idea is to become joyfully and totally exhausted. Then at the moment of orgasm (and not a split second before) let the Magician remember the purpose of the operation (the Skrying of the Æthyr) and repeat the first line of the Call; **Madariatza das perifa TEX cahisa micaolazoda saanire caosago od fifsa balzodizodarasa Iaida.** This may be done verbally or mentally but it must be well memorized so that it can come forth effortlessly.

(Note: A tape recorder can be used for both repeating Calls and taking notes. Sometimes two recorders are very handy, one for taking notes and the other for playing Calls).

The Magician then falls exhausted and allows the flood of images to wash through his brain. The temptation to fall asleep will be almost irresistible and that is where the skill of the Assistant is most vital.

After a few quiet moments if the Magician is not relating his vision to the Assistant she must take it upon herself to question him. This requires a high degree of tact and subtlety for she does not want to disturb the vision and yet she cannot allow him to fall into a deeper state of unconsciousness. This takes practice. She should have a pad of paper and a pencil handy and should write down everything that the Magician says. She should be especially careful to correctly spell any unknown words or phrases and she should not hesitate to ask the Magician (or the entity speaking through the Magician) the correct spelling of Angelic words.

If the vision stalls and reaches a point where nothing further is happening the Assistant can sometimes give it a push.

EXAMPLE

Magician: All I see is a bunch of trees. Nothing is happening.

Assistant: Try turning around. Do you see anything now?

Magician: Just more trees but there is a small pond in the middle.

Assistant: Walk over to the pond. Look in the pond and tell me what you see.
Magician: At first I see only my own reflection but as I keep looking I see that the pond is actually a bowl supported by the wings of four Angels. etc.

If angels or other beings appear in the vision they must be tested by repeating the names of the Governors one at a time. If the entity shows discomfort at the name of any of the Governors dismiss it by continuing to repeat the Governor's name until it disappears and a being appears that is strengthened by hearing the names.

Do not be afraid of anything you "see" or "hear". Maintain an attitude of good natured tolerance even if hideous sights or terrifying beings or creatures appear. Act like a dispassionate explorer. *Fear is failure and the forerunner of failure.*

When it is clear that the vision is finished, or when it is obvious that the Magician is now fatigued or ready to fall asleep it is time to end the operation.

It is of the utmost importance that the Magician now "snap out of it" for it is he who must banish and close the Temple. If the Magician is reluctant to "wake up" and perform his duties it is the Assistant's responsibility to *see that he does*. No effort should be spared to "break the spell" and return the Magician to the objective world. Turn on the lights, talk loudly, get a drink, or splash some water on your face.

Finally, he performs the Lesser Banishing Ritual of the Pentagram and the Magician and the Assistant review the notes and transfer them to the Magician's diary. The comments of the Assistant are often extremely important and should not be omitted in the record.

Often the couple will wish to change roles and explore the same Æthyr on a subsequent occasion. Allow at least one day between operations.

EXPLORATION OF THE ELEMENTAL UNIVERSE AND CREATION OF THE MAGICKAL CHILD

Dr. Israel Regardie believed that certain Sex Magick techniques could be used by advanced students to incarnate "spiritual" energies on the physical plane, as well as making important shifts in the orientation of the Psyche and the Universe. In other words, if these methods were used properly, couples could bring into the world "divine" forces in the children they generated, who could influence the future of the race.

In addition to creating "real children" these methods could be used to create "bio-psycho-spiritual vessels", which would shift the focus of the mind as well as develop new powers and abilities.

The creation of the magickal child by ritualized sexual practices is symbolic in one sense of the whirling forces of nature, mixing and separating in their chaotic dance of creation.

This mixing and separating process is vividly displayed in the Elemental Tablets and the Tablet of Union of the Enochian system. Working with these basic forces of nature allows conscious co-operation and co-creating with the cosmos, and the magician becomes a miniature form of the cosmic process following its root law.

By willful and conscious co-operation the magician increases and refines his energies, sacrificing himself or herself willingly to Nature instead of being a passive food source in the spiritual food chain. The realization that man's emotional, physical and sexual energies are food for the "gods" can create great personal turmoil at first, however when one begins to joyously participate in the spiritual feeding frenzy, one is "elevated perpendicularly to infinity."

SELECTING THE MAGICKAL CHILD
THE ENOCHIAN METHOD

The selection process is the most difficult and, in truth, the most magickal, aspect of the operation. The "soul searching" necessary for such an important act is awesome and should not be embarked upon with a frivolous attitude.

The Enochian adept (and no other should embark upon such project) is intimately familiar with every area of the Elemental environment and with his or her current initiatory position relative to the Thirty Æthyrs. By reviewing his or her personal diaries of perhaps hundreds of non sexual Enochian workings, the Magician can determine the areas of the system that manifest the qualities which are desirable in the magickal child.

For the purpose of our illustration we will say that we wish create a magickal child of purity and beauty. A child capable of reflecting and transmitting energy and impressions without being affected. A child such as this might be a great actor or politician because in this child others see themselves reflected. This is charming and disarming to others because when they look at the child they will see only what they want to see.

By checking the records of our previous evocations we see that **TDIM**, the Kerub ruling the *Water* Subangle of *Water* is the perfect Spirit to manifest in such a child.

The technique as outlined below has been adapted from the exercise The Orgastic Circulation of Light and is an excellent example of Tantric Enochian evocation.

In Dr. Regardie's copy of Wilhelm's *Secret Of The Golden Flower,* 3rd impression, 1935, there are a number of passages underlined. Dr. Regardie was not a habitual underliner, thus we may assume that when he did underline it was for a very good reason. One of the passages which he underlined more than once contained references to the circulation of light.

In the next method, the proper circulation of light is essential for true magickal effects to occur and has been modified for use in creating the magickal child. It is urged that the partners should practice the ritual many times *prior* to including the sexual aspects. As a rule it is wise to practice this together holding hands or touching in some fashion.

At the time determined most auspicious for the conception of the magickal child the Temple is made ready, Banished, Cleansed and Consecrated.

The Temple is then opened in the Grade of 3°=8 as outlined in *Chanokh* and the two participants recite a brief Oath declaring their intention to perform this creative act.

PART I
THE GREAT WHIRLINGS

The male should be on his back and the female should sit on top of him. Move only when instructed, unless the penis begins to lose its stiffness.

Begin by imagining a *scintillating white light* about the size of a small basketball forming above the head and piercing the top of the skull. This is called the Kether point. Now vibrate the Three Holy Names of God (from the Water Tablet). **MPH ARSL GAIOL** as the sphere of Light grows brighter and more energetic. Do this for five minutes.

On the last six vibrations of **MPH ARSL GAIOL** the female should move on each sound of the Names.

As the force of this whirling ball of power becomes exceedingly real for you and your partner, allow the energy to descend slowly through the head. Allow it to rest in the throat or Da'ath point. Here imagine a *lavender color*. Vibrate the Name of the Great Elemental King of Water, **RAAGIOSL** until the energy becomes exceedingly real for you and your partner.

Again on the last six vibrations of **RAAGIOSL** the female should move six times.

Bring the energy down through the chest until it rests at the Heart or Tiphareth. Vibrate the Names of the six Seniors of the Water Tablet, **SAIINOV, SOAIZNT, LAOAZRP, LIGDISA, SLGAIOL, LSRAHPM**. The color of light should be *golden yellow* growing brighter and clearer as you vibrate each Name.

On the six last vibrations of the names of the Seniors the female should move six times.

Move the power through the diaphragm and abdominal region to the pelvis (Yesod), and vibrate the Divine Names of the Calvary Cross, Water of Water, **NELAPR**, **OMEBB** visualizing a sphere of *deep purple*.

Here on the last ten vibrations of **NELAPR** and **OMEBB** the male should move ten times very slowly.

Finally, allow the energy to descend through the legs until it formulates at Malkuth, the feet. Both participants vibrate the name of the Kerub, the Name of their magickal child **TDIM** visualizing a *black* sphere.

The male should again move ten times quickly on the final vibrations of the Child's name.

Now, draw the energy up from the Black light of Malkuth changing colors as described above as it ascends to Kether. When the light reaches Kether concentrate on the White brilliance of this region.

When the light is at Kether and your movements are complete, meditate silently for a few moments and then begin the circulation of white light.

Note: At times Dr. Regardie ignored the different colors of the Spheres and simply used the white scintillating light of Kether for each of the points. However, he and I agreed that the colored system is better suited for the practice of Sex Magick.

PART II
THE ORGASTIC CIRCULATION OF LIGHT

Circulate the energy of the White Light as follows:

Allow it to descend downward and outward via the left side of the body during every exhalation. When it reaches the left foot, transfer the energy over to the right foot and allow it to ascend the right side of the body on the inhalation. This should be done at least 10 times. The partners should move slowly in unison 10 times.

The second circulation of energy begins in Kether and travels down the front of the body on the exhalation and then up the back of the body on the inhalation. This should be done at least ten times as well. The partners should move slowly in unison ten times.

The third circulation, beginning with Kether follows down through the body on the exhalation until it reaches Malkuth. The energy is drawn up through the body to Kether on the inhalation. When it reaches the Crown, imagine it to discharge like water from a fountain, at the end of each inhalation. The fire and sparks of this scintillating fountaining go up and out through the Crown and then descend down and encompasses the body on the exhalation. After the final circulation has been completed and the fountaining maintained for a few movements, the couple should begin moving and breathing heavily as they surround themselves with sparkling light. The movements should then become spontaneous and at the moment of orgasm the light should be gathered and thrust beyond Sahasrara, toward the Chakkra with No Name.

PART III
THE CRYSTALLIZATION OF THE LIGHT

The orgastic Light of the Chakkra of No Name may be likened to the Philosopher's Stone, The Golden Flower, or the Lotus. It is a body of light created by the process of transmutation of spiritual-sexual energy and is the womb of the magickal child. This is an experiential realization, thus, the proof of the pudding is in the Doing and Creating.

The process of transmutation requires the proper balance and mixing of heat and cold, passive and active, and white and black. In a broader sense we are using tremendous active forces to create a non-active force. The nurturing we provide the womb-child through our practices creates a worthy resting place of deep silence for the aspirants involved in the creation process.

The circulating of orgastic light is no doubt one of the most beautiful secrets of the Great Work. As the light circulates again and again and your practices become more powerful

Taboo: The Ecstasy Of Evil

and refined, a crystallization occurs and you begin to form the magickal child. Whether you choose it to be physical or spiritual or both, the creation of this spirit body allows you to have contact with the forces of the higher Spiritual Body. You have not only opened the doors of perception, but can now begin the process of real action in a way unknown to those who lack this initiation.

CHAPTER THIRTY THREE

BIBLICAL EROTICA

One does not need to be a Biblical scholar to recognize the sexual facets of many Bible stories. The Bible is filled with examples of sexual behavior, attitudes and mythology.

Stories of miraculous pregnancies are particularly interesting to the Sex Magician as they relate to a fundamental and classic technique whereby spiritual entities are consciously incarnated. If one compares the stories surrounding the births of Khrishna and the Buddha with those of Isaac, John the Baptist and Jesus, one sees striking similarities which to the Sex Magician can reveal profound clues to the true nature of both God and Man.

The Song of Songs (more accurately translated "The Greatest of all Songs") is unique among the Books of the Bible. Attributed to Solomon and placed after Ecclesiastes in the Greek Bible, and between Ecclesiastes and the Book of Wisdom in the Latin Vulgate, it is the first of the five works traditionally recited by the Jews at Passover and other great feasts.

What makes all this unusual is that it is not even remotely characteristic of any other book of the Bible. It is a series of love poems—passionate and explicitly erotic.

Jewish scholars of the First Century A.D. argued that such literature did not belong in the sacred canon but were overruled by the more conservative factions who maintained that its popularity and antiquity necessitated its continued inclusion as sacred scripture. This appeal to tradition has kept it part of the Bible of the Christian Church as well.

Once resigned to the "Holiness," of the Song of Songs, Jewish and Christian scholars alike have endeavored to assign "appropriate" parochial interpretations to the work. Commentators have gone to almost comical lengths to show that the lovers are really God and Israel or that Christ desires to climb his Church like a palm tree and seize its breasts as a cluster of grapes.

Making the 'simple' complex and making the 'obvious' obscure has long been a primary occupation of not only religious scholars but of academicians, and practicing physicians as well. They use language to cloud meaning and, if projected with sufficient authority, assure themselves a monopoly on thought.

We have included below the entire text of The Song of Songs and ask the reader to put it in perspective with the material found earlier in this book concerning sexual union with the divine. If after you have read it, you feel that it has nothing to do with the sexual aspects of religion then we are afraid you have pulled the wool over your own eyes.

THE SONG OF SONGS
Attributed to Solomon the King

The Song of Songs, which is Solomon's

The Bride

Let him kiss me with the kisses of his mouth.
Your love is more delightful than wine;
delicate is the fragrance of your perfume,
your name is an oil poured out,
and that is why the maidens love you.
Draw me in your footsteps, let us run.
The King has brought me into his rooms;
you will be our joy and our gladness.
We shall praise your love above wine;
how right it is to love you.

FIRST SONG OF LOVE

The Bride

I am black but lovely, daughters of Jerusalem,
like the tents of Kedar,
like the pavilions of Salmah.
Take no notice of my swarthiness,
it is the sun that has burnt me.
My mother's sons turned their anger on me,
they made me look after the vineyards.
Had I only looked after my own!

Tell me then, you whom my heart loves:
Where will you lead your flock to graze,
where will you rest it at noon?
That I may no more wander like a vagabond
beside the flocks of your companions.

The Chorus

If you do not know this, O loveliest of women,
follow the track of the flock
and take your kids to graze
close by the shepherd's tents.

The Bridegroom

To my mare harnessed to Pharaoh's chariot
I compare you, my love.
Your cheeks show fair between their pendants
and you neck within its necklaces.
We shall make you golden earrings
and beads of silver.

Discourse of the Bride and Bridegroom

—While the King rests in his own room

my nard yields its perfume.
My beloved is a sachet of myrrh
lying between my breasts.
My Beloved is a cluster of henna flowers
among the vines of Engedi.

—How beautiful you are, my love,
how beautiful you are!
Your eyes are doves.

—How beautiful you are, my Beloved,
and how delightful!
All green is our bed.

—The beams of our house are of cedar,
the panelling of cypress.

—I am the rose of Sharon,
the lily of the valleys.
—As a lily among the thistles,
so is my love among the maidens.
—as an apple tree among the trees of the orchard,
so is my Beloved among the young men.
In his longed-for shade I am seated
and his fruit is sweet to my taste.
He has taken me to his banquet hall,
and the banner he raises over me is love.
Feed me with raisin cakes,
restore me with apples
for I am sick with love.
His left arm is under my head,
his right embraces me.

—I charge you,
daughters of Jerusalem,
by the gazelles, by the hinds of the field,
not to stir my love, nor rouse it,

until it please to awake.

SECOND SONG OF LOVE

The Bride

I hear my Beloved.
See how he comes
leaping on the mountains,
bounding over the hills.
My Beloved is like a gazelle,
like a young stag.

See where he stands
behind our wall.
He looks in at the window,
he peers through the lattice.

My Beloved lifts up his voice
he says to me
'Come then, my love,
my lovely one, come.
For see, winter is past,
the rains are over and gone.
The flowers appear on the earth.
The season of glad songs has come,
the cooing of the turtledove is heard
in our land.
The fig tree is forming its first figs
and the blossoming vines give out their fragrance.
Come then, my love,
my lovely one, come.
My dove, hiding in the clefts of the rock,
in the coverts of the cliff, show me your face,
let me hear your voice;
for your voice is sweet
and you face is beautiful.

Taboo: The Ecstasy Of Evil

Catch the foxes for us,
the little foxes that make havoc of the vineyards,
for our vineyards are in flower.

My Beloved is mine and I am his.
He pastures his flock among the lilies.

Before the dawn-wind rises,
before the shadows flee,
Return! Be my Beloved,
like a gazelle,
a young stag,
on the mountains of the covenant.

On my bed, at night, I sought him
whom my heart loves.
I sought but did not find him.
So I will rise and go through the City,
in the streets and the squares
I will seek him whom my heart loves.
...I sought but did not find him.

The watchmen came upon me
on their rounds in the City:
'Have you seen him whom my heart loves?

Scarcely had I passed them
than I found him whom my heart loves.
I held him fast, nor would I let him go
till I had brought him
into my mother's house,
into the room of she who conceived me.

The Bridegroom

I charge you,
daughters of Jerusalem,

by the gazelles, by the hinds of the field,
not to stir my love, nor rouse it,
until it please to awake.

THIRD SONG OF LOVE

What is this coming up from the desert
like a column of smoke,
breathing of myrrh and frankincense
and every perfume the merchant knows?

See, it is the litter of Solomon.
Around it are sixty champions,
the flower of the warriors of Israel;
all of them skilled swordsmen,
veterans of battle.
Each man has his sword at his side,
against alarms by night.

King Solomon
has made himself a throne
of wood from Lebanon.
The posts he has made of silver,
the canopy of gold,
the seat of purple;
the back is inlaid with ebony.

Daughters of Zion,
come and see
King Solomon,
wearing the diadem with which his mother crowned him
on his wedding day,
on the day of his heart's joy.

The Bridegroom

How beautiful you are, my love,

Taboo: The Ecstasy Of Evil

how beautiful you are!
Your eyes, behind your veil,
are doves;
your hair is like a flock of goats
frisking down the slopes of Gilead.
Your teeth are like a flock of shorn ewes
as they come up from the washing.
Each one has its twin,
not one unpaired with another.
Your lips are a scarlet thread
and your words enchanting.
Your cheeks, behind your veil,
are halves of pomegranate.
Your neck is the tower of David
built as a fortress,
hung round with a thousand bucklers,
and each the shield of a hero.
Your two breasts are two fawns,
twins of a gazelle,
that feed among the lilies.

Before the dawn-wind rises,
before the shadows flee,
I will go to the mountain of myrrh,
to the hill of frankincense.

You are wholly beautiful, my love,
and without a blemish.

Come from Lebanon, my promised bride,
come from Lebanon, come on your way.
Lower your gaze, from the heights of Amana,
from the crests of Senir and Hermon,
the haunt of lions,
the mountains of leopards.

You ravish my heart,

my sister, my promised bride,
you ravish my heart
with a single one of your glances,
with one single pearl of your necklace.
What enchantments lie in your love,
my sister, my promised bride!
How delicious is your love, more delicious than wine!
How fragrant your perfumes,
more fragrant than all other spices!
Your lips, my promised one,
distill wild honey.
Honey and milk
are under your tongue;
and the scent of you garments
is like the scent of Lebanon.

She is a garden enclosed,
my sister, my promised bride;
a garden enclosed,
a sealed fountain.
Your shoots form an orchard of pomegranate trees,
the rarest essences are yours:
nard and saffron,
calamus and cinnamon,
with all the incense-bearing trees:
myrrh and aloes,
with the subtlest odors.
Fountain that makes the gardens fertile
well of living water,
streams flowing down from Lebanon.

The Bride

Awake, North Wind,
come, Wind of the South!
Breathe over my garden,
to spread its sweet smell around.

Let my Beloved come into his garden,
let him taste its rarest fruits.

The Bridegroom

I come into my garden,
my sister, my promised bride,
I gather my myrrh and balsam,
I eat my honey and my honeycomb,
I drink my wine and my milk.
Eat, friends, and drink,
drink deep, my dearest friends.

FOURTH SONG OF LOVE

The Bride

I sleep, but my heart is awake.
I hear my Beloved knocking.
'Open to me, my sister, my love,
my dove, my perfect one,
for my head is covered with dew,
my locks with the drops of night.
—'I have taken off my tunic,
am I to put it on again?
I have washed my feet,
am I to dirty them again?
My beloved thrust his hand
through the hole in the door;
I trembled to the core of my being.
Then I rose
to open to my Beloved,
Myrrh ran off my hands,
pure myrrh off my fingers,
on to the handle of the bolt.

I opened to my Beloved,

but he had turned his back and gone!
My soul failed at his flight.
I sought him but I did not find him.
I called to him but he did not answer.
The watchmen came upon me
as they made their rounds in the City.
They beat me, they wounded me,
they took away my cloak,
they who guard the ramparts.

I charge you,
daughters of Jerusalem,
if you should find my Beloved,
what must you tell him...?
That I am sick with love.

The Chorus

What makes your Beloved better that other lovers,
O loveliest of women?
What makes your Beloved better than other lovers,
to give us a charge like this?

The Bride

My Beloved is fresh and ruddy,
to be known among ten thousand.
His head is golden, purest gold,
his locks are palm fronds
and black as the raven.
His eyes are doves
at a pool of water,
bathed in milk,
at rest on a pool.
His cheeks are beds of spices,
banks sweetly scented.
His lips are lilies,

distilling pure myrrh.
His hands are golden, rounded,
set with jewels of Tarshish.
His belly a block of ivory
covered with sapphires.
His legs are alabaster columns
set in sockets of pure gold.
His appearance is that of Lebanon,
unrivalled as the cedars.
His conversation is sweetness itself,
he is altogether lovable.
Such is my Beloved, such is my friend,
O daughters of Jerusalem.

The Chorus

Where did your Beloved go,
O loveliest of women?
Which way did your Beloved turn
so that we can help you to look for him?

The Bride

My Beloved went down to his garden,
to the beds of spices,
to pasture his flock in the gardens
and gather lilies.
I am my Beloved's, and my Beloved is mine.
He pastures his flock among the lilies.

FIFTH SONG OF LOVE

The Bridegroom

You are beautiful as Tirzah, my love,
fair as Jerusalem.
Turn your eyes away,

for they hold me captive.
Your hair is like a flock of goats
frisking down the slopes of Gilead.
Your teeth are like a flock of sheep
as they come up from the washing.
Each one has its twin,
not one unpaired with another.
Your cheeks, behind your veil, are halves of pomegranate.

There are sixty queens
and eighty concubines
(and countless maidens).
But my dove is unique,
mine, unique and perfect.
She is the *darling of her mother,*
the favorite of the one who bore her.
The maidens saw her, *and proclaimed her blessed,*
queens and concubines sang her praises:
'Who is this arising like the dawn,
fair as the moon, resplendent as the sun,
terrible as an army with banners?

I went down to the nut orchard
to see what was sprouting in the valley,
to see if the vines were budding
and the pomegranate trees in flower.
Before I knew…my desire had hurled me
on the chariots of my people, as their prince.
The Chorus

Return, return, O maid of Shulam,
return, return, that we may gaze on you!

The Bridegroom

Why do you gaze on the maid of Shulam
dancing as though between two rows of dancers?

Taboo: The Ecstasy Of Evil

How beautiful are your feet in their sandals,
O prince's daughter!
The curve of your thighs is like the curve of a necklace,
work of a master hand.
Your navel is a bowl well rounded
with no lack of wine,
your belly a heap of wheat surrounded with lilies.
Your two breasts are two fawns,
twins of a gazelle.
Your neck is an ivory tower.
Your eyes, the pools of Heshbon,
by the gate of Bath-rabbim.
Your nose, the Tower of Lebanon,
sentinel facing Damascus.
Your head is held high like Carmel,
and its plaits are as dark as purple;
a king is held captive in your tresses.
How beautiful your are, how charming,
my love, my delight!
In stature like the palm tree,
its fruit-clusters your breasts.
'I will climb the palm tree,' I resolved,
"I will seize its clusters of dates.
May your breasts be clusters of grapes,
your breath sweet-scented as apples,
your speaking, superlative wine.

The Bride

Wine flowing straight to my Beloved,
as it runs on the lips of those who sleep.
I am my Beloved's
and his desire is for me.
Come, my Beloved,
let us go to the fields.
We will spend the night in the villages,
and in the morning we will go to the vineyards.

We will see if the vines are budding,
if their blossoms are opening,
if the pomegranate trees are in flower.
Then I shall give you
the gift of my love.
The mandrakes yield their fragrance,
the rarest fruits are at our doors;
the new as well as the old,
I have stored them for you, my Beloved.

Ah, why are you not my brother,
nursed at my mother's breast!
Then if I met you out of doors, I could kiss you
without people thinking ill of me,
I should lead you, I should take you
into my mother's house, and you would teach me!
I should give you spiced wine to drink
juice of my pomegranates.

His left arm is under my head
and his right embraces me.

The Bridegroom

I charge you,
daughters of Jerusalem,
not to stir my love, nor rouse it,
until it please to awake.

THE CONCLUSION

The Chorus

Who is this coming up from the desert
leaning on her Beloved?

The Bridegroom

Taboo: The Ecstasy Of Evil

I awakened you under the apple tree,
there where your mother conceived you,
there where she who gave you birth conceived you.

Set me like a seal on your heart,
like a seal on your arm.
For love is strong as Death,
jealousy relentless as Sheol.
The flash of it is a flash of fire,
a flame of Yahweh Himself.
Love no flood can quench,
no torrents drown.